The Historical Eye

THE HISTORICAL EYE

The Texture of the Visual
in Late James

SUSAN M. GRIFFIN

Northeastern University Press
BOSTON

Northeastern University Press

Copyright 1991 by Susan M. Griffin

Library of Congress Cataloging-in-Publication Data

Griffin, Susan M., 1953–
    The historical eye : the texture of the visual in late James / Susan M. Griffin.
        p.   cm.
    Includes bibliographical references and index.
    ISBN 1-55553-092-3
    1. James, Henry, 1843–1916—Knowledge—Psychology. 2. James, Henry, 1843–1916—Criticism and interpretation. 3. Visual perception in literature. 4. Psychology in literature. I. Title.
PS2127.P8G7   1991   90-46999
813′ .4--dc20

Designed by Ann Twombly

This book was composed in Bembo by Impressions, Inc., in Madison, Wisconsin. It was printed and bound by Maple Press, York, Penn. The paper is Sebago Antique Cream, an acid-free sheet.

MANUFACTURED IN THE UNITED STATES OF AMERICA
95 94 93 92 91   5 4 3 2 1

To my parents, Doris Kenah and John Michael Griffin

Contents

Figures

Acknowledgments

DURING THE LONG MAKING of this book, friends, colleagues, and family have been generous with time, energy, ideas, expertise, and support. Throughout, my family has been steadfast with encouragement and assistance. While working at the University of Chicago on the dissertation that was the genesis of this book, I received advice and direction from James E. Miller, Jr., Robert E. Streeter, Diana Postlethwaite, and Robert J. Richards. Scott Teissler's introduction to word processing proved indispensable. Bob Ferguson and Beth Helsinger were extremely helpful as my research moved beyond the graduate stage. At the University of Louisville, Bill Axton, Bob Miller, Tom Byers, and Lucy Freibert gave advice and support. Financial assistance from the University of Louisville's Arts and Sciences Research Committee and the Commission on Academic Excellence were essential to the completion of this project, as was the work of Beth Basham and Peggy Strain, my research assistants. I also received support from the University Committee on Academic Publication. Steve Melville and Dale

Bauer read the manuscript in draft and made a number of useful suggestions. Richard A. Hocks, along with another, anonymous, reader for Northeastern University Press reviewed the manuscript carefully and generously; the book is a better one thanks to their recommendations. Bill Frohlich's commitment to academic publishing, his personal engagement in the making of books, has earned my deep respect. My greatest debts are to William Veeder and Douglas R. Sharps. I am afraid to count the number of times each has read some part or version of this work since its inception. At its best, this book incorporates their words, meets their objections, reflects their thought.

I use the following editions for works frequently cited:

Henry James

The American Scene (Bloomington: Indiana University Press, 1968).

The Art of Criticism: Henry James on the Theory and the Practice of Fiction, ed. William Veeder and Susan M. Griffin (Chicago: University of Chicago Press, 1986), abbreviated *AC*.

The Art of the Novel: Critical Prefaces (1934; reprint, Boston: Northeastern University Press, 1984), abbreviated *AN*.

Henry James Letters, ed. Leon Edel, 4 vols. (Cambridge: Harvard University Press, 1974–84), cited by correspondent, date, volume and page numbers.

Literary Criticism, vols. 2 and 3 of *Henry James* (New York: Literary Classics of the United States, 1984), abbreviated *HJLC* and cited by volume and page number.

The Novels and Tales of Henry James, 26 vols. (New York: Charles Scribner's Sons, 1907–17), cited by volume and page numbers.

"Winchelsea, Rye, and 'Denis Duval' " in *English Hours* (1905; reprint, London: Oxford University Press, 1981).

"Within the Rim" in *Within the Rim and Other Essays, 1914–1915* (London: W. Collins Sons, 1918).

Other Authors

William James, *The Principles of Psychology*, Works of William James, ed. Frederick Burkhardt, 3 vols. (Cambridge: Harvard University Press, 1981), cited by volume and page numbers.

John Ruskin, *The Complete Works of John Ruskin*, ed. E. T. Cook and Alexander Wedderburn, 39 vols. (London: George Allen, 1903–12), cited by volume and page numbers.

The Historical Eye

Introduction

AS MY TITLE IMPLIES, *The Historical Eye* is part of the current critical movement to rehistoricize our reading of Henry James. Michael Anesko has pointed out that, because James's "twentieth-century revival coincided with the evolution of modernist sensibility," the "James" that became canonical was an isolated, ivory tower aesthete whose fictions stood aloof from historical and material circumstance.[1] Despite recent attempts to place his life and work in its familial and literary contexts, understanding of James remains hampered by the acceptance of two critical commonplaces rooted in that modernist sensibility: the idea that his fictional world is structured by a dichotomy between observation and experience and the notion that the Jamesian protagonist is a "passive observer," a cerebral, almost disembodied, being, completely detached from the world of experience. Situated at a moment in James criticism when a new historicism and poststructuralist theory have together prompted rereadings of both Henry James's texts and the phenomenon of "Henry James," *The Historical Eye* seeks to reexamine the stock figure of the Jamesian perceiver.

3

My topic is *visual perception*: what James's characters, and later, James himself as a character, are described as actually seeing. This focus on the physical eye contextualizes James's work in several ways. James's analysis of perception is informed by the psychological and aesthetic theories of his day. Further, as seeing bodies, James's characters are firmly located in a temporal, spatial environment. And what the Jamesian perceiver sees is not only historically constituted, it is itself historical. Like the landscape painters and art critics whose works instructed his eye, James and his characters focus on the visible traces of time. Finally, studying James's representations of seeing alters our understanding of his literary context, allowing us to recognize his functionalism as a reworking of the associationist tradition and thus to rethink his connections to American nativism.

Recognition of the fact that Jamesian visual perception is a process that takes place in and over time reveals much about the structure of James's writing as well. The histories of James's perceivers inform both the temporal nature of their identities and the shape of James's own narration. For James, character *is* fictional structure.[2] His narrative strategies are intimately tied to his understanding of his characters' positions as creatures, and creators, of their worlds and their selves, a relation that is spelled out in the visual interactions between the two.

The Jamesian eye's historicity is a human—indeed, a Jamesian—construction. For James, "history" is not a body of determined and determining facts, but a text. The literary, aesthetic, and psychological traditions that James claims as his own are appropriated from and for the present, a present that is also a textured construction. Jamesian history is an explicit topic in Chapters 3 and 4 of my study, which explore James's recognition that the identities of nations and persons, of literary works and words, are temporal creations. Like William James, for whom personal identity is a "relative" (1:352)[3] entity in constant flux, Henry is interested, not in some "real," prior self, but in the *experience* of identity over time. In his descriptions of the visual interplay between self and environment, we can trace the making of these historical identities. And the perceptual stream wherein James constructs—and reconstructs—his own historical self displays his ambivalent participation in the political and economic conditions that surround him.

By making this Jamesian idea of history both the subject and the methodology of my study, I seek to avoid the determinism that has flawed some recent "new historicist" criticism.[4] Rather than reading James as an historical effect or result, I demonstrate how the interactive, creative process of Jamesian perception provides an alternative model for a literary historicism, one that recognizes James as both written by, *and* writing, history.

In its textualizing of Jamesian psychology through a contextualizing of Jamesian perception, *The Historical Eye* looks forward. Both phenomenological and poststructuralist critics have been drawn to Henry James's writing, reading James through, and as, literary theory. Studying William and Henry James's analytic accounts of eye and I in their turn-of-the-century context represents a step toward the historicizing of such readings. As Paul B. Armstrong, John Carlos Rowe, Bruce Wilshire,[5] and others have pointed out, William James directly influenced Edmund Husserl in particular and phenomenology in general; Husserl's philosophy of language, in turn, evokes Derrida's critical rereading, serving as an important early text for deconstruction.[6] Particularly in Chapter 4, when I examine Henry James's perceptual analyses of representation and signification, my study has benefited from the ways in which the scene and thematics of writing have been foregrounded in recent literary criticism and theory. However, *The Historical Eye* diverges from deconstructionist readings in a number of ways, most prominently in my emphasis on the visual over the verbal and in my insistence that Jamesian perception is a physical process. Crucial to my historical resituating of the body of James's work is the resituation of the body in his works. Yet to recognize the eye as a bodily organ is not, of course, to claim that seeing in James can be understood without regard to language. The process of perception is linguistically represented in James's text; further, as Chapter 1 demonstrates, Jamesian visual perceptions are never pure sensations but, rather, textured by verbal, aural, and tactile associations. Nonetheless, the visual is so important a *medium* of thought for James that it saturates his writing. James's characterization of John Singer Sargent's talent illustrates the ways in which the visual can entail a kind of representational logic: "Perception with him is already by itself a kind of execution. . . . The process by which the object seen resolves itself into the object pictured is extraordinarily immediate. It is as if painting were pure tact of vision, a simple manner of feeling."[7] Informing, at times almost impelling, James's literary representations is what John La Farge recognized as his "painter's eye."

The Historical Eye begins by analyzing Jamesian seeing in light of turn-of-the-century psychology.[8] Primary among the visual studies upon which I draw is William James's *Principles of Psychology*. The reason for my reliance on William James is the obvious one: the two brothers, while often in disagreement, conversed, corresponded, recommended and exchanged articles and books, and read one another's works throughout their lives. Indeed, for Henry, it was a relationship that survived even William's death in 1910: "But he is a possession, of real magnitude, and I shall find myself still living upon him to the end. My life, thank God, is impregnated with him."[9] Leon Edel's five-volume life of the novelist argues that William and Henry's sibling rivalry is *the* interpretive key to both brothers' lives. While Edel's claim has been contested, there is no disagreement about the existence of what Howard M. Feinstein calls a "fraternal bond . . . of long standing . . . fostered by closeness in age, shared aesthetic interests, and the constant deracination of their childhood" and "their shared fate as the earliest subjects of their father's educational experiments."[10] As the brothers matured, their styles of living and writing seem to have diverged radically: Henry, the man of letters, living in Europe and remaining single, developing increasingly complex, "difficult" fictions; William, psychologist, philosopher, and family man, teaching and writing in America, attempting always "to say a thing in one sentence as straight and explicit as it can be made, and then to drop it forever."[11] However, as Richard A. Hocks has pointed out, to focus on this stylistic divergence is to miss Henry's sustained interest in William's work.[12] In response to what was perhaps William's harshest critique of a Henry James novel (*The Golden Bowl*), his brother replied, "And yet I can read *you* with rapture. . . ."[13]

The reason for this "rapture" has been suggested in studies connecting William's philosophy and Henry's fiction, foremost among these Hocks's *Henry James and Pragmatistic Thought*.[14] Although Hocks's topic is "thought," not perception, the fact that William James's philosophy grows directly out of his psychology means that Hocks's discussion of the streamlike, active nature of Jamesian mental processes lays the groundwork for my analysis of the stream of seeing in James. Discussions of Henry's writing that address directly its connections to William's *psychology* have been more limited, perhaps because of a critical reluctance to recognize affinities between the art of fiction and the materials—and materiality—of science.[15] Yet as scholars like Gillian Beer and Sally Shuttleworth have shown, "All novelists in the nineteenth century were inevitably affected by the close interdependence of social and scientific thought."[16] Scientists wrote in language accessible to educated lay readers, often drawing upon literary examples. Indeed, as Beer points out, our use of "the term 'lay-man' to describe the relationship of a non-scientist to the body of scientific knowledge" is relatively new.[17] Victorian science was "a shared, cultural discourse."[18] Robert M. Young has argued that by the late nineteenth century increasing special-ization and professionalization indicate that this "common in-tellectual context" was breaking down.[19] Nonetheless, much of William James's *Principles of Psychology* was published first, not only in *Mind* and *The Journal of Speculative Philosophy*, but also in *Popular Science Monthly* and *Scribner's*. (The last pub-lished Henry James's work as well.) And, while it remains uncertain whether Henry made his way completely through *The Principles of Psychology*, we do know that he read several of these articles.[20] However, in studying the connections be-tween the two James brothers' perceptual psychologies, I am not arguing that the theories of William James and others are consciously applied in Henry James's practice. I will be reading the brothers' writings next to one another, not in order to prove direct influence, but for a more pragmatic reason: the structures and language of turn-of-the-century psychology al-low us to uncover the workings of Henry James's characters' perceptions.[21] These perceivers confront the problems, and en-act the solutions, central to the psychology of James's time. As George Levine points out, "Novels are not science; but both incorporate the fundamental notions of the real that dom-inate the culture."[22] William and Henry share the same task: "The mind which the psychologist studies is the mind of dis-tinct individuals inhabiting definite portions of a real space and of a real time."[23]

Understanding how William James's psychological theories of perception illuminate Henry James's fiction requires our recognition that, in 1890, this description of the psychologist's task is new—as is psychology itself. The primary context for the Jamesian eye is the redefinition of both mind and its study in which William James participates. Before turning to analysis of Jamesian perception, therefore, I will outline the nature of psychology's turn-of-the-century revolution.

The uncertainty of psychology's early disciplinary standing is indicated by the fact that until 1886 it was subsumed under "Metaphysics" in the *Encyclopaedia Britannica*. In that year, James Ward's essay "Psychology," published as a separate entry, declared the field's status as a science whose subject matter included both brain and mind. Ward goes on to describe his field's focus: "Psychology . . . never transcends the limits of the individual. . . . It is not enough to talk of feelings or volitions: what we mean is that some individual, man or worm, feels, wills, acts—thus or thus."[24] This statement is echoed in William James's contention that the psychologist's task is the study of "distinct individuals" and reflected in the work of Francis Galton and James McKeen Cattell, who, partly as a result of Darwin's discussions of the variations within species, created a psychology of individual differences. The new recognition of the individual *as* psychological context was coupled with an insistence that the individual be studied *in* context. William James's post-Darwinian recognition that a mental *"faculty does not exist absolutely, but works under conditions"* led to the argument that "bodily experiences . . . and more particularly brain-experiences, must take a place amongst those conditions of the mental life of which Psychology need take account" (1:17–18).

It is these historical changes in the nature of the discipline that present the strongest argument for studying Henry James's work within a psychological, rather than a philosophical, context. His literary revision of the terms and structures of realism and his psychological redefinition of character, plot, and setting coincide with psychology's reconstitution of itself as the study of individual minds in concrete circumstances.

Both Ward and James are arguing for a psychology based in functionalism.[25] Functionalist psychology can perhaps best be understood as a reaction to, and revision of, associationism. The associationist school, whose origins were Aristotelian, and whose systematization is usually credited to Hartley and Hume, had dominated eighteenth- and early nineteenth-century studies of the mind. Associationist psychologists described a mental life comprised of discrete sensations. The mind was merely a *tabula rasa*, a place where these atoms of sensation combined and recombined. Therefore, only units of sensation, not individual subjects, were the objects of psychological investigation.

Literary criticism of British writers from Sterne to Wordsworth has benefited greatly from the study of associationist psychology.[26] And, as scholars like William Charvat, Terence Martin, and Donald A. Ringe have shown, associationist psychology, by way of Common Sense philosophy, actually helped provide a critical rationale for an American literature.[27] Associationism's literary influence is generally agreed to have extended from the eighteenth through the early nineteenth century in England and slightly later in America. Romantic notions of the self, it is argued, then began to displace associationism in literary circles.[28] However, many readings of later writers like James, while not directly concerned with psychological models, rest on generally associationist principles. The notion that James's characters are "passive observers" is based upon such assumptions: perceivers are the passive recipients of atomistic sensations.[29]

The functionalist challenge to associationism, issued in articles like William James's 1884 "On Some Omissions of Introspective Psychology" in *Mind* and James Ward's 1886 *Encyclopaedia Britannica* essay, was

> the beginning of a new attitude toward the problems of mind. The article [Ward's] clearly challenged the Associationists to show cause why they should continue to exist. No one wished to deny the value of the laws of

Association as true for some aspects of consciousness and some of its connections; the question here put to the issue was whether 'association' should be regarded as the bedrock of all mental complexity and unity, or whether it was a minor affair dependent upon some larger and deeper conception of unity.[30]

While acknowledging the explanatory power of the associative mechanism, functionalists attempted to alter the study of the mind in light of Darwin's discoveries. "After Darwin, biologists saw each anatomical structure of an organism as a functioning element in an integrated and successful living system."[31] Functionalists argued that psychology must begin to understand the mind in just this way, as "an organ, which, like any other organ, has been evolved for the benefit of its possessor."[32] Indeed, in the first chapter of *The Principles of Psychology*, William James contends that the mind *is* its function: "*The pursuance of future ends and the choice of means for their attainment are thus the mark and criterion of the presence of mentality* in a phenomenon. . . . *No actions but such as are done for an end, and show a choice of means, can be called indubitable expressions of Mind*" (1:21, 23). The language of Henry James's Prefaces, where he characterizes his own thought processes as, variously, an explorer's search, the dragging of a river, and a bloodhound's hunt, echoes this functional definition of mind.[33]

William James's description of mental activity is incompatible with the associationist model of perception, which described atomistic sensations impinging upon a passive subject and building into larger units of perception. Functionalists argued that psychology should study *subjects*, not units of sensation. William James corrects the associationist abstraction of isolated mental building blocks:

Most books start with sensations, as the simplest mental facts, and proceed synthetically, constructing each higher stage from those below it. But this is abandoning the empirical method of investigation. No one ever had a simple sensation by itself. Consciousness, from our natal day, is of a teeming multiplicity of objects and relations, and what we call simple sensations are results of discriminative attention, pushed often to a very high degree. . . . Every thought tends to be part of a personal consciousness. (1:219–20)

By insisting that mental events cannot be understood apart from their complex, personal contexts, functional psychology provides a structure for understanding Henry James's literary contention that "there is no such thing in the world as an adventure pure and simple; there is only mine and yours, and his and hers—it being the greatest adventure of all, I verily think, just to *be* you or I, just to be he or she."[34] Psychology's shift in focus from sensation to subject is mirrored, as Chapter 3 will show, in the move from the literary associationism of Bryant, Cooper, and Irving to the functionalist textuality of Jamesian perception.

Functionalism's emphasis on context is external as well as internal.[35] The subjects that William James describes are to be analyzed, not in isolation, but *functionally*, as products and producers of histories and environments. As William James emphasizes, it is crucially important to study a mind in its milieu:

On the whole, few recent formulas have done more real service of a rough sort in psychology than the Spencerian one that the essence of mental life and of bodily life are one, namely, 'the adjustment of inner to outer relations.' Such a formula is vagueness incarnate; but because it takes into account the fact that minds inhabit environments which act on them and on which they in turn react; because, in short, it takes mind in the midst of all its concrete relations, it is immensely more fertile than the old-fashioned 'rational psychology,' which treated the soul as a detached existent, sufficient unto itself, and assumed to consider only its nature and properties. (1:19)

Spencer's insistence upon placing the organism in its environment is, however, flawed for James by its assumption that "inner" relations passively adjust to outer events. The functionalists contended that subjects are active, not passive, in nature, that they alter, as well as adjust to, their environments.[36] Sensation, perception, attention, reasoning, aesthetic creation, ethical thought—all entail active mental selection. Through interest, we create our world. "We may, if we like, by our reasonings unwind things back to that black and jointless continuity of space and moving clouds of swarming atoms which science calls the only real world. But all the while the world *we* feel and live in will be that which our ancestors and we, by slowly cumulative strokes of choice, have extricated out of this, like sculptors, by simply rejecting certain portions of the given stuff" (1:277).

For the functionalist, an active subject selects its perceptions in the course of an interested, changing relation with its undifferentiated environment. And it does so in order to survive. The question of an organism's survival in its environment may seem, at best, tangential to a study of Henry James's fiction. As he made clear in the Preface to *The Princess Cassamassima*, for James, "Experience . . . is our apprehension and our measure of what happens to us as social creatures" (*AN*, 64–65). However, evolutionary and functional psychology did not confine itself to primitive behavior. The environment that interests both James brothers is the social environment of civilized society. Few of William James's examples of self-interested survival involve food or fire. Dealing with highly sophisticated social beings, his discussion of the "self" touches upon intellectual interests, concern about "club-opinion," and love of fine, clean clothing. Because he contends that the material Self, the social Self, the spiritual Self, and the pure Ego are all basic *"constituents of the Self"* (1:280), his analysis captures the complexity of civilized human behavior. And it is in this very complexity that danger lies: a self that is constituted socially is dependent upon, and limited by, others.

Accordingly, in exploring the tactics of human survival, William James does not restrict his discussion to tooth and claw. Instead, he argues that consciousness itself is the functional result of evolution. The sophisticated flexibility of human consciousness allows its "possessor to adapt his conduct to the minutest alterations in the environing circumstances, any one of which may be for him a sign, suggesting distant motives more powerful than any present solicitations of sense" (1:142). Moving from the safe predictability of reflexes to these finely tuned responses entails risks: "A low brain does few things, and in doing them perfectly forfeits all other use. The performances of a high brain are like dice thrown forever on a table" (1:143). What this risky situation means is that as "*a fighter for ends*" consciousness may opt for indirect action and deferred results (1:144). Our notions of "survival," William James stresses, must include the realization that a higher consciousness actually *creates* its own interests (1:143–44). Henry James's minute examinations of the indirect, subtle, movements of the mind and eye have often been read as signs of an overly refined aesthetic disdain for the practical bases of "real life." William James's explanation shows that "basic" need not mean "crude," that Henry's subtleties and indirections are themselves highly functional aspects of the self's interested relationship with its environment.[37]

As late nineteenth-century psychologists turned from the examination of isolated "ideas" to the study of a mind immersed in a physical environment and a personal history, they faced the problem of determinism. The dilemma can be (and was) clearly articulated in perceptual terms: If external environment dictates visual reaction, our world creates us; we can only react in ultimately predictable ways. If internal pattern predetermines how the environment is seen and perception is merely mechanical, the past may blind us to the present.

William James tries throughout *The Principles* to reconcile his belief in free will with his Darwinian conviction that humans are engaged in an adaptive relation with their surroundings. Surprisingly, James finds in evolutionism itself justifications for a belief in the indeterminacy of human behavior. He argues that "chance variation" introduces the possibility of spontaneity, the possibility that the cosmos is not a great clock whose motions are mechanical and determined.[38]

More significant for Henry's fiction is the fact that William also finds strong indications of indeterminacy in the mind's interested relationship with its environment. He postulates that, if free will exists, it can be located in moments of attentive perception. James explains in detail how attention is, above all, interested. He says that "what-we-attend-to and what-interests-us are synonymous terms" (2:1164). What we perceive is thus determined functionally, by our needs. The biological nature of attention is, then, rather than a proof of simple determinism, the possible source of our ability to choose our perceptions. Thus, his focus on the *activity* of the subject.

According to William James, associationism, by focusing on sensations and relegating the subject to the role of passive receiver, had virtually ignored this potential source of individual power:

> So patent a fact as the perceptual presence of selective attention has received hardly any notice from the psychologists of the English empiricist school.... In the pages of such writers as Locke, Hume, Hartley, the Mills, and Spencer the word hardly occurs, or if it does so, it is parenthetically and as if by inadvertence. The motive of this ignoring of the phenomenon of attention is obvious enough. These writers are bent on showing how the higher faculties of the mind are pure products of 'experience'; and experience is supposed to be of something simply *given*. Attention, implying a degree of reactive spontaneity, would seem to break through the cir-

cle of pure receptivity which constitutes 'experience,' and hence must not be spoken of under penalty of interfering with the smoothness of the tale. (1:380)

By regarding creatures as "absolutely passive clay, upon which 'experience' rains down," writers like Spencer overlook the way subjective interest "*makes* experience more than it is made by it" (1:381). For William James, we are "sculptors," not clay (1:277).

In correcting this passive picture of experience, William James does not do away with association. Association takes place, whether we will it or not, and attention cannot, therefore, grant complete freedom of action. We may direct our attention and thus select and compose our perceptions, but the potential objects of both attention and perception are limited. Our pasts, our bodies, and our environments work together to present us with a range of possible perceptions. "But even though there be a mental spontaneity, it can certainly not create ideas or summon them *ex abrupto*. Its power is limited to *selecting* amongst those which the associative machinery has already introduced or tends to introduce" (1:559).

Although we can only choose from among those ideas that the associative machinery sets before us, such acts of attention are crucial. Despite the power of the past implied by perception's mechanical associationist basis, neither James brother ultimately describes seeing deterministically. "If it [mental spontaneity] can emphasize, reinforce, or protract for a second . . . it can do all that the most eager advocate of free-will need demand; for it then decides the direction of the next associations by making them hinge upon the emphasized term; and determining in this wise the course of the man's thinking, it also determines his acts" (1:559). Negligible as this momentary power may sound, it is, nonetheless, as James explains, "*morally and historically momentous*" (2:1180). In fixing our attention for even a second, we determine the direction of our next associations. We choose which personal interests will direct our behavior. We act.

William James's disciplinary engagement with the question of free will reflects an anxiety pervasive in Victorian culture. As a writer of narratives, Henry James also faced the problem of determinism. In the narrative structure offered by an associationist model, character is created by the passive, sequential build-up of experience. These "evolutionary narratives," as Gillian Beer calls them, show the past clearly and straightforwardly determining the present, beginnings leading inexorably to their ends.[39] This is precisely the fictional pattern implicit in Zola's naturalist definitions of character and description—"The character has become the product of the air and the soil, like a plant. . . . I should define description: 'An account of the environment which determines and completes man.' "[40] The perceptual passivity and narrative predictability that result can be seen at their most extreme in a novel like *McTeague*, where Norris catalogs a series of sights presented to a character. After listing each detail of the scene outside McTeague's window, the narrator notes that "day after day, McTeague saw the same panorama unfold itself." These are the units of sensation that build up to shape the passive McTeague. The recognition that the history of a character's engagement with his or her environment *is*, precisely, that character is clearly reflected in the shape of the naturalist plot.

While Henry James shares the realist/naturalist interest in exploring the relations between characters and their environments, he differs in that he describes those relationships as active and reciprocal. Rather than denying the relentless chronology of the self's material history, Henry James, like his brother, grounds the possibility of freedom in the body, of the I in the eye.[41] Traceable in the spatial textures of Jamesian perception are the temporal strategies of his perceivers and the narrative structures of his texts. Interestingly selecting present perceptions, attentively choosing among possible associations, actively remembering, rather than merely passively repeating, the past, the functional self moves back and forth in time. With such a model available to him, James can construct narratives in which the history of a character is not an undeviating chronology of sensations passively experienced. Just as the functional self is simultaneously creator and creature of its environment, so is it also producer and product of its own history.[42]

If chronological determinism represents one danger for James's perceivers, the disruption of the relations among past, present, and future offers an opposing threat. The possibility of a break in the temporal integrity of the self seemed, for a variety of historical reasons, particularly real to James's contemporaries. The discoveries of natural science in general and of Darwin in particular created "a newly intensified sense of evanescence associated with concepts of geological time, of extinction, and of irreversible and random genetic mutation" and implied that "oblivion is prospective as well as past, universal as well as individual."[43] In addition, as Alexander Welsh has shown, the information revolution, the rise of publicity, and the concept of circumstantial evidence all helped to focus Victorians on "the continuity and discontinuity of personal histories."[44] Given this cultural context, we can recognize Jamesian seeing as an active, interested struggle both to create *and* to preserve the self.

His visual efforts to sustain an identity over time reveal that "character" is "story" for James in a double sense. Not only does psychology structure James's plots, but Jamesian identity itself is narrative. Especially in later writings when "James" is presented as perceiver, the visual provides a medium in which to construct accounts of the self.[45] The function, and functionalism, of Jamesian visual perception becomes all the clearer when James himself, faced with the destruction of the American landscape of his youth, World War I's threat to the English countryside that has become his home, and the approach of his own death, struggles to see the sights that will permit "Henry James" to survive.

The various narrative implications of functionalism account for *The Historical Eye*'s focus on late James. Although functionalist elements appear in James's earliest fiction, it is only in his later work that visual perception is fully functional. While none of James's early writings are strictly deterministic, they are influenced by Balzac's and Zola's attempts to describe the universal laws that shape human character.[46] As James moves away from these influences and into the psychological plotting of the late phase, his explorations of the relations between character and environment begin to resemble more closely the functionalist model of an actively engaged subject, creating a self and choosing a history. These activities are quite literally given body in James's characters' visual perceptions.[47]

Chapter 1, "The Selfish Eye: Strether's Principles of Psychology," outlines the basic mechanics of Jamesian visual perception, using as an example the character generally regarded as James's prototypical perceiver: Lambert Strether in *The Ambassadors*. William James's stream of consciousness provides the primary model for an understanding of how Strether sees. In defining the nature of the perceptual stream, I explore the complex relationship between the visual and the verbal in Henry James's writing. Perception is, William James implies, structured like a language. Strether's stream of perception constitutes a system of visual signs. While his past sights and his present material situation dictate the grammar of his visual images, within these constraints perceptual activity is still possible. In the visual texts created by Strether's interactions with his environment we can trace his perceptual survival tactics: discrimination, analysis, attention. Strether directs his vision toward what interests him, and what interests him is what he needs to see. To recognize his selfish eye is not to condemn Strether but to acknowledge the conditions of Jamesian perception.

"The Opening Door: Seeing the Self in *The Golden Bowl*" analyzes visual perception in James's last novel. Maggie Verver sees as Strether does, yet her perceptions diverge from his in a number of ways: the Princess often struggles to achieve her sights; her mental images are frequent and important; and these external and internal sights are directed toward the attainment of a social self-consciousness. Functional psychology again proves useful in the analysis of these perceptions. In particular, William James's studies of mental images and of the structure of the self illuminate what Maggie sees. However, the relationship between James's work and psychology shifts in this chapter. Having used *The Ambassadors* as a source of examples in order to place Jamesian seeing in a larger context, I now reverse my emphasis and show how an understanding of the functional nature of Jamesian perception helps us to read a James novel, *The Golden Bowl*. *The Golden Bowl* has been recognized as a novel about power;[48] analysis of Maggie's perceptions allows us to anatomize the negotiated structures of power in James's text. Maggie's sights, whether structured domestic scenes or mental images that appear and reappear, reveal her growing awareness of herself as both creature and creator of her social environment. When the identity of the self is a function of the social environment, when knowledge is both visually acquired and displayed, seeing and being seen become strategies in the struggle to survive. Maggie's visual power demonstrates that the gaze is not exclusively male in James.[49] Social relations and the perceptual exchanges that enact them are profoundly gendered, but the female is neither denied, nor spared, the power of knowledge.

Nor does James spare himself. The second half of *The Historical Eye* focuses on James's nonfiction as the site for a perceptual construction of a self. Criticism in general, and James studies in particular, have in recent years abandoned their traditional exclusive focus on canonical "literary" texts. Scholars like Carol Holly, David Furth, Mutlu Konuk Blasing, and William Veeder have uncovered the literariness of James's autobiographical, travel, and even critical writings;[50] at the same time, literary theory has prompted the investigation of "Henry James" as an historical, rhetorical construction.[51] Tracing James's perceptual negotiations with his spatial, temporal environments continues this inquiry into the authoring of Henry James. Identifying the active functionalism of these visual transactions allows us to recognize James as both authored and author, enables us to follow Carolyn Porter's suggestion that we begin to read literary texts as "participating in a cultural conversation rather than merely re-presenting the conclusion reached in that conversation. . . ."[52]

Chapter 3 traces the perceptual strategies of self-preservation in the visual landscape of *The American Scene*. James represents himself as following Strether's functional pattern of perception; however, because he is looking at landscape, he also draws on his wide knowledge of painting and aesthetics in order to picture America. This chapter therefore supplements the psychological model of seeing with perceptual theories drawn from the visual arts.

In *The American Scene*, James selects his own artistic history, a history that differs from those constructed by later critics. He appropriates the associationist spectator so central to the work of the Hudson River painters and early American writers, transforming this traditional type into a more active, functional perceiver. The Jamesian ability to visually "read" landscapes comes partly from his study of Ruskin, himself an important influence in American art. However, James's twentieth-century engagement with the arts of his childhood is not an act of nostalgia. On the contrary, it is his urgent concern about

America's future that prompts James to draw upon Hudson River paintings. He explicitly demonstrates how the flatness of contemporary painting cannot serve his needs, at the same time rejecting generalized, "classic" European landscapes in favor of detailed, localized American scenes, filled with an atmospheric, iridescent depth.[53]

Studying James's American scenes as landscapes also reveals his encounters with the problems indigenous to the genre. Trying to picture an America that has not erased the past, James confronts his attitudes toward nature and culture. Precariously balanced between these two realms are the Arcadian scenes where James struggles to visually integrate personal, literary, and cultural history, to see a temporalized space, capable of accommodating narration. Yet what these visual chronicles reveal is that James's death, too, haunts Arcadia.

James's interest in locating himself as the perceiver of an historical American landscape is fueled by his identity as a narrative artist and frustrated by his position as a twentieth-century American. The early chapters of *The American Scene* reveal a growing sense of perceptual dislocation. Attempting to see the human story in the landscape, James risks falling into detached visual consumption of the American scene. Because he sees historically, James participates, despite himself, in the very commodification of America that he condemns. My delineation of James's cultural complicity works against an assumption that, as Walter Benn Michaels has argued in *The Gold Standard and the Logic of Naturalism*, underlies the bulk of American literary criticism: the idea that great literature must stand outside of, and in opposition to, consumer culture. In contrast, Michaels's analysis demonstrates the way the work of writers like Dreiser participates in, and even exemplifies, commodity culture.[54] The final visual perception in *The American Scene* is similarly exemplary. Having purchased with his railway window seat the "awful modern privilege of this detached yet concentrated stare at the misery of subject populations," James sees his native land through the plate glass of consumerism.

In the process of perceiving the American landscape, then, James performs an historical analysis of the self, an analysis that gradually blocks his visual entry into the American scene. Chapter 4, "The Architecture of the Jamesian Eye: Home as Seen" describes James's perceptual attempts to identify an alternative, English self. These attempts center around East Sussex, where Lamb House is located and where England's island boundary lies visible. The visual excursions into East Sussex in "Winchelsea, Rye, and 'Denis Duval' " (1901) explore the fundamentally literary nature of both "James" and the landscape that houses him. As he cycles between Winchelsea and Rye, James's changing vantage points reveal him as complexly double: an adult writer remembering himself as a youthful reader. Constructing perceptual pictures of the landscape, he investigates the textual encounters between readers and writers and between past and present selves over time. If James rewrites literary history in *The American Scene*, in "Winchelsea, Rye, and 'Denis Duval' " he italicizes representation.

By 1914, James's political situation is such that visual, literary, and mnemonic structures seem about to dissolve. In "Within the Rim," James faces the disruption of identity: World War I threatens to violate both the "England" and the "Henry James" that he has known. Forced, like Maggie, into self-consciousness, James attempts to reidentify himself through a perceptual reconstruction of the English landscape. To retain continuity while incorporating change is, for James, to narrate, and it is precisely the narrative nature of identity which his 1914 landscapes display. What the Great War also reveals is the historicity of these accounts of identity. Not only the stories of "James" and "England," but also the images and words that compose them, exist "in the circumstances." The circumstances of 1914 are so discontinuous with the past that signification itself seems at risk. Strether's visual stream shows that perception is structured like a language; "Within the Rim" demonstrates that Jamesian language, whether visual or verbal, is historical.

Notes

1. Michael Anesko, *"Friction with the Market": Henry James and the Profession of Authorship* (New York: Oxford University Press, 1986), vii.

2. See, for example, "The Art of Fiction" and the Preface to *The Portrait of a Lady* (*AC*, 165–96, 286–99).

3. Unless otherwise noted, all William James references are to *The Principles of Psychology*.

4. Although most new historicists explicitly attempt to avoid historical determinism as well as formalism (largely through a post-structuralist reading of "history"), they have been charged with both. See, for example, Edward Pechter, "The New Historicism and Its Discontents: Politicizing Renaissance Drama," *PMLA* 102 (1987): 292–303, and Carolyn Porter's assessment of both Pechter and the new historicists, "Are We Being Historical Yet?" *South Atlantic Quarterly* 87 (1988): 743–86.

5. Paul B. Armstrong, *The Phenomenology of Henry James* (Chapel Hill: University of North Carolina Press, 1983), 3–4; John Carlos Rowe, *Henry Adams and Henry James: The Emergence of a Modern Consciousness* (Ithaca: Cornell University Press, 1976), 37–38; Bruce Wilshire, *William James and Phenomenology: a Study of "The Principles of Psychology"* (Bloomington: Indiana University Press, 1968), 3–8.

6. See Jacques Derrida, *Speech and Phenomena and Other Essays on Husserl's Theory of Signs*, trans. David B. Allison (Evanston: Northwestern University Press, 1973).

7. "John S. Sargent" in *The Painter's Eye*, ed. John L. Sweeney (1956; reprint, Madison: University of Wisconsin Press, 1989), 217.

8. Sharon Cameron's *Thinking in Henry James* (Chicago: University of Chicago Press, 1989), which I encountered as this book was going to press, argues that "James dissociates consciousness from psychology" (1), thus disputing directly the usefulness of any such turn to the history of psychology. I will not attempt to summarize

Cameron's subtle and complex argument here, noting only that despite this fundamental methodological disagreement, our studies do focus on some of the same aspects of James's writing: see Cameron's discussions of the ways Jamesian consciousness exists *between* persons, of seeing in James as interactive, of how Jamesian thinking can be said to be visible, and her brief remarks on James's literary life after death.

9. Letter to H. G. Wells, 11 September 1910 (4:562).

10. Howard M. Feinstein, *Becoming William James* (Ithaca: Cornell University Press, 1984), 224.

11. Letter to Henry James, 4 May 1907, in *Letters of William James*, ed. Henry James, 2 vols. (Boston: Atlantic Monthly Press, 1920), 2:277.

12. Richard A. Hocks, *Henry James and Pragmatistic Thought: A Study in the Relationship between the Philosophy of William James and the Literary Art of Henry James* (Chapel Hill: University of North Carolina Press, 1974), 4.

13. Letter to William James, 23 November 1905 (4:383).

14. Because Hocks's concerns are philosophical, not psychological, his focus is on how William James's pragmatism is opposed to *a priori* reasoning. Thus Hocks often stresses Henry James's characters' freedom, whereas my emphasis is on the way individuals' psychological, biological, and physical structures, as well as their environments, limit that freedom.

15. Two studies, Judith Ryan, "The Vanishing Subject: Empirical Psychology and the Novel," *PMLA* 95 (1980): 857–69, and, more recently, Michael S. Kearns, *Metaphors of Mind in Fiction and Psychology* (Lexington: University of Kentucky Press, 1987), focus explicitly on William James's psychology. Both in their general arguments about the connections between nineteenth-century literature and psychology and at specific points in their discussions of Henry and William James, Ryan's and Kearns's studies parallel my own. However, Ryan's focus on a literary "movement away from narration through the medium of a specific subjective mind to a technique in which, as Virginia Woolf puts it, 'the world is seen without a self' " (857) causes her to minimize the functional aspects of Jamesian psychology. Kearns's demonstration that there is a general movement in nineteenth-century literature and psychology from the metaphor of "mind-as-entity" to that of the mind as a sentient web is not focused on the visual, and his discussion of Henry James maintains a tradi-

tional, and, as I will argue, mistaken, distinction between "sensations" and "knowledge" (199).

16. Gillian Beer, *Darwin's Plots: Evolutionary Narrative in Darwin, George Eliot and Nineteenth-Century Fiction* (London: Routledge and Kegan Paul, 1983), and Sally Shuttleworth, *George Eliot and Nineteenth-Century Science: The Make-Believe of a Beginning* (Cambridge: Cambridge University Press, 1984). The quote is from Shuttleworth who, unfortunately, begins her book by misreading James's criticism of *Middlemarch*'s "echo of Messrs. Darwin and Huxley" as a "dogmatic distinction between the realms of art and science" (ix). However, she goes on to describe James as "a writer whose novels were themselves suffused with the notions of nineteenth-century science" (ix). See also Kearns's claim that George Eliot and Henry James "imbibed on a daily basis the most advanced psychological theories and discoveries of their time" (179). On James and science, see Alexander Welsh, "Theories of Science and Romance, 1870–1920," *Victorian Studies* 17 (December 1973): 135–54, and Strother B. Purdy, *The Hole in the Fabric: Science, Contemporary Literature, and Henry James* (Pittsburgh: University of Pittsburgh Press, 1977).

17. Beer, *Darwin's Plots*, 7.

18. George Levine, *Darwin and the Novelists: Patterns of Science in Victorian Fiction* (Cambridge: Harvard University Press, 1988), 3.

19. Robert M. Young, "Natural theology, Victorian periodicals, and the fragmentation of a common context," in *Darwin's Metaphor: Nature's Place in Victorian Culture* (Cambridge: Cambridge University Press, 1985), 126–64.

20. For evidence of Henry's reading of William's psychological writings, see his letters to William on 14 November 1878 (2:192–94); to Mrs. Henry James, Sr., on 18 January 1879 (3:210–14); to William on 1 October 1887 (3:198–205); to William on 7 November 1890 (3:304–6); to William on 6 February 1891 (3:328–31).

21. See Hocks, *Henry James:* "I am proposing essentially that William James's pragmatistic thought is literally *actualized* as the literary art and idiom of his brother Henry James, especially so in the later work" (4).

22. Levine, *Darwin and the Novelists*, 13.

23. William James, 1:183. See Shuttleworth, *"Middlemarch*: An experiment in time," in *George Eliot*, 142–74, for the argument that *"Middlemarch* is a work of experimental science: an examination of the 'history of man' under the 'varying experiments of Time' (Pre-

lude, I, 1)" (143). While his study is largely unconcerned with connections between fiction and the historical discipline of psychology, Gordon O. Taylor, *The Passages of Thought: Psychological Representation in the American Novel, 1870–1900* (New York: Oxford University Press, 1969), astutely describes how "roughly between 1870 and 1900 fictive psychology in the American novel undergoes a fundamental shift . . . toward a concept of organically linked mental states requiring representational emphasis on the nature of the sequential process itself. . . . The basic frame of reference . . . has become concretely environmental; mind is assumed to be physiological, and the development of narrative as well as the shaping of fictive issues depends on its response to environmental stimuli" (5–6).

24. "Psychology" *Encyclopaedia Britannica*, vol. 20 (New York: Charles Scribner's Sons, 1886), 38, 39.

25. In psychology, the term "functionalism" is used to designate both a formal school of thought, centered at the University of Chicago under John Dewey and James R. Angell, and a more widespread general movement in psychology after Darwin. I am using functionalism in the latter sense.

26. For important early examples, see John Traugott, *Tristram Shandy's World: Sterne's Philosophical Rhetoric* (Berkeley: University of California Press, 1954), and Arthur Beatty, *William Wordsworth: His Doctrine and Art in Their Historical Relations* (Madison: University of Wisconsin Press, 1922).

27. William Charvat, "Sources in Scottish Philosophy, Aesthetics, and Culture," in *The Origins of American Critical Thought: 1810–1835* (Philadelphia: University of Pennsylvania Press, 1936), 27–58; Terence Martin, *The Instructed Vision: Scottish Common Sense Philosophy and the Origins of American Fiction* (Bloomington: Indiana University Press, 1961); Donald A. Ringe, *The Pictorial Mode: Space and Time in the Art of Bryant, Irving, and Cooper* (Lexington: University of Kentucky Press, 1971). See also William P. Hudson, "Archibald Alison and William Cullen Bryant," *American Literature* 12 (March 1940): 59–68; Robert E. Streeter, "Association Psychology and Literary Nationalism in the *North American Review*, 1815–1825," *American Literature* 17 (1945): 243–54; James T. Callow, *Kindred Spirits: Knickerbocker Writers and American Artists, 1807–55* (Chapel Hill: University of North Carolina Press, 1967); and Robert A. Ferguson, "William Cullen Bryant: The Creative Context of the Poet," *New England Quarterly* 53 (December 1980): 431–63.

28. M. H. Abrams, *The Mirror and the Lamp: Romantic Theory and the Critical Tradition* (New York: Oxford University Press, 1953).

29. For a direct argument that Jamesian psychology is associationist, see J. H. Raleigh, "Henry James: The Poetics of Empiricism," in *Henry James: Modern Judgements*, ed. Tony Tanner (London: Macmillan and Company, 1968), 52–66.

30. George Stanley Brett, *Brett's History of Psychology*, ed. and abr. R. S. Peters (New York: The Macmillan Company, 1953), 642.

31. Richard J. Hernstein and Edwin G. Boring, "Functionalism," in *A Source Book in the History of Psychology* (Cambridge: Harvard University Press, 1965), 482.

32. Ibid. See also Roger Smith, "The Human Significance of Biology: Carpenter, Darwin, and the *vera causa*," in *Nature and the Victorian Imagination*, ed. U. C. Knoepflmacher and G. B. Tennyson (Berkeley: University of California Press, 1977), 216–30.

33. See, respectively, the Prefaces to *Roderick Hudson*, *The American*, and *The Ambassadors* (*AC*, 259–70, 271–85, 361–75).

34. "The Lesson of Balzac," (*HJLC* 3:135).

35. As subsequent discussion will show, self and environment are mutually, interactively created in James; thus, a sharp distinction between "external" and "internal" is impossible. I use the terms in a non-strict sense here to connote the line that the individual draws between the world and the self, between what William James calls the "not-me" and the "me" (1:278).

36. Phillip Wiener, *Evolution and the Founders of Pragmatism* (1949; reprint, Philadelphia: University of Pennsylvania Press, 1972), 102–4.

37. See Hocks, *Henry James*, 95–98, on "The 'Democracy' of Henry James."

38. John C. Greene, *The Death of Adam: Evolution and Its Impact on Western Thought* (Ames: Iowa State University Press, 1959), 305–6, and Robert J. Richards, "The Personal Equation in Science: William James's Psychological and Moral Uses of Darwinian Theory," *Harvard Library Bulletin* 30 (October 1982): 387–425.

39. Beer, *Darwin's Plots*: "At first evolutionism tended to offer a new authority to orderings of narrative which emphasised cause and effect, then, descent and kin. Later again, its eschewing of fore-ordained design (its dysteleology) allowed chance to figure as the only sure determinant" (8). See also Levine, *Darwin and the Novelists*, 16–19, 191–201, on Darwinian, character-generated narratives as opposed to conventional, teleological plots.

40. Emile Zola, "The Critical Formula Applied to the Novel," in *The Naturalist Novel*, ed. Maxwell Geismar (Montreal: Harvest House, 1964), 86.

41. On this topic, see my discussion of *The Ambassadors* in Chapter 1. Debates about free will in Henry James's fiction often discuss *The Ambassadors*, but generally center around the passage in which Strether himself describes "the affair of life" as "a tin mould . . . into which, a helpless jelly, one's consciousness is poured" (21:218) and do not take into account the ways James represents perception and attention.

42. "James never tires of demonstrating the extent to which the self is identical with what the self perceives, is in fact created by the very act of perceiving" (Ryan, "The Vanishing Subject," 861).

43. Gillian Beer, "Origins and Oblivion in Victorian Narrative," in *Sex, Politics, and Science in the Nineteenth-Century Novel*, ed. Ruth Bernard Yeazell (Baltimore: Johns Hopkins University Press, 1986), 65–66. Beer goes on to claim that "through geology, prehistory, the extension of the past, the insistence in evolutionary ideas on change and loss of nameable origins, the forgetting and deforming of meaning in language, the debilitating of memory as an agent of transformation and control in Darwinian theory—through all these factors, together with a common insistence on growth, the Victorians were made to be aware of how much was irretrievably forgotten, and to set great store by those signs and traces, those acts of decipherment that relieved oblivion and reconstituted themselves as origins" (84–85).

44. Alexander Welsh, *George Eliot and Blackmail* (Cambridge: Harvard University Press, 1985), 20.

45. Like all Jamesian perceivers, "James" is a literary construction. However, for the sake of typographical simplicity, I drop the quotation marks in ensuing discussions. Chapter 4 explicitly discusses James on both the social texture of the writer's identity and the narrative nature of identity in general.

46. On the early influence of French writers on James, see Lyall J. Powers, *Henry James and the Naturalist Movement* (East Lansing: Michigan State University Press, 1971), and Phillip Grover, *Henry James and the French Novel: A study in inspiration* (New York: Barnes and Noble, 1973).

47. This emphasis on the visual as the primary means of rendering the interactions between the self and its environment is also a feature

of the late phase. For example, James's most important early rendering of a mind thinking—Chapter 42 in *The Portrait of a Lady*—is primarily nonvisual. *The Historical Eye* thus contests the critical tradition that reads the stylistic changes of the late phase as evidence of James's retreat from a "real-world" environment. A recent (Lacanian) reworking of this traditional reading is Donna Przybylowicz, *Desire and Repression: The Dialectic of Self and Other in the Late Works of Henry James* (Tuscaloosa: The University of Alabama Press, 1986), who argues that in the middle period James "concentrates on the protagonist's intersubjective relationships in the natural-fact-world, while the late writings portray vividly the individual's intrasubjective experience and confrontation with in a realm of Imaginary specularity" (4).

48. See, e.g., Mark Seltzer, *Henry James and the Art of Power* (Ithaca: Cornell University Press, 1984).

49. An essential discussion of the male gaze is Laura Mulvey, "Visual Pleasure and Narrative Cinema," *Screen* 16 (Autumn 1975): 6–18. See Judith Mayne, "Feminist Film Theory and Women at the Movies," *Profession 87*: 14–19, for a concise sketch of the ways in which recent feminist film theorists like Teresa DeLauretis and others have attempted to deconstruct the categories of male spectator and female object, and Craig Owens, "The Discourse of Others: Feminists and Postmodernism" in *The Anti-Aesthetic: Essays on Postmodern Culture*, ed. Hal Foster (Port Townsend, Wash.: Bay Press, 1983), 57–82, on similar deconstructive effects in the postmodernist works of some female visual artists.

50. See, Carol Holly, "A Drama of Intention in Henry James's Autobiography," *Modern Language Studies* 13 (1983): 22–31; David Furth, *The Visionary Betrayed: Aesthetic Continuity in Henry James's The American Scene* (Cambridge: Harvard University Press, 1979); Mutlu Konuk Blasing, "The Story of the Stories: Henry James's Prefaces as Autobiography" in *Approaches to Victorian Autobiography*, ed. George P. Landow (Athens: Ohio University Press, 1979), 311–32; William Veeder, "Image as Argument: Henry James and the Style of Criticism," *Henry James Review* 6 (1985): 172–81. See also my "James's Revisions of 'The Novel in "The Ring and the Book," ' " *Modern Philology* 85 (1987): 57–64.

51. See, for example, John Carlos Rowe, *The Theoretical Dimensions of Henry James* (Madison: University of Wisconsin Press, 1984).

52. Porter, "Are We Being Historical Yet?" 782. Although I find Porter's language congenial here, my study clearly does not answer her call for a more political, more Marxist new historicism.

53. As Chapter 3 will make clear, my argument about the nature of the visual in *The American Scene* is unrelated to the question of whether or not James is a "literary impressionist" or, for that matter, a "literary Hudson River painter." I am not claiming that the literary techniques used to create *The American Scene* resemble the methods employed in painting a picture, nor that the experience of reading James's text is anything like that of viewing a painting, nor that the spatialization of time in these scenes entails what has come to be known as *novelistic* "spatial form." Instead, I show that James describes himself as perceiving landscapes very much like those pictured in nineteenth-century American paintings.

54. Walter Benn Michaels, *The Gold Standard and the Logic of Naturalism: American Literature at the Turn of the Century* (Berkeley: University of California Press, 1987). See also Seltzer's Foucauldian reading of Jamesian cultural power in *Henry James and the Art of Power.*

CHAPTER I

The Selfish Eye

Strether's Principles of Psychology

LAMBERT STRETHER of *The Ambassadors* has long been acknowledged as the prototypical Jamesian perceiver[1] and, indeed, attributes of Strether's vision are characteristic of seeing
in James. By portraying Strether's perceptions as functional,
James contextualizes his character both spatially and temporally: what Strether sees ties him to the physical world that
surrounds him and to the past that he carries within him. At
the same time, the active, interested, attentive nature of functional perception means that in the act of seeing, Strether
shapes his world and his past. Visual perception is a means by
which he struggles to survive in and over time. Understanding
perception's role in the survival of Strether's self means understanding more fully how seeing can constitute a complex,
active, analytic engagement with the environment. The very
structure of Jamesian visual perception—that of a unified
stream—illustrates the fullness and intricacy of Strether's interactions with his world.

Active and interested as Strether's visual efforts are, his
seeing is restricted by both his immediate environment and

the history of his relations with his world. In attempting to see what he needs to see, Strether must contend not only with Chad's and Marie's visual manipulations, but also with his own perceptual past. Strether cannot eliminate these material, social, and temporal constraints, but, by learning and attending visually, he can limit them. I will analyze both Strether's environmental restrictions and the visual survival tactics with which he combats them below. In order to do so, however, we need to examine more closely the structure of Strether's seeing.

Yeazell outlines the reasons that Jamesian characters have seemed removed from earthy and unstructured processes like the "stream of consciousness":

> To a modern reader, long accustomed to the idea that much of consciousness operates below the level of language, the very look of a Jamesian meditation on the page suggests a mind in which the intellect is very much in control. For the unconscious does not, we suspect, obey the rules of grammar and of syntax, and James's men and women think in sentences which no more resemble the unpunctuated flow of words in Molly Bloom's final monologue or the bizarre strings of neologisms in *Finnegans Wake* than their sleeping habits resemble those of Joyce's rather drowsy characters. Though the Jamesian sentence strains, it does not break: no stream of consciousness, the critics all agree, flows through the pages of James's late fiction.[2]

Henry James does not write in what literary critics have defined as "stream of consciousness." Indeed, the psychologist who originated the phrase, William James,[3] argues that the full intricacy of the "stream of consciousness" can never be completely recreated. Nonetheless, William James consistently uses the arrangement of the grammatically correct sentence to represent the structure of the stream:

> As we take, in fact, a general view of the wonderful
> stream of our consciousness, what strikes us first is this
> different pace of its parts. Like a bird's life, it seems to
> be made of an alternation of flights and perchings. The
> rhythm of language expresses this, where every thought
> is expressed in a sentence, and every sentence closed by
> a period. The resting-places are usually occupied by sen-
> sorial imaginations of some sort, whose peculiarity is that
> they can be held before the mind for an indefinite time,
> and contemplated without changing; the places of flight
> are filled with thoughts of relations, static or dynamic,
> that for the most part obtain between the matters con-
> templated in the periods of comparative rest. (1:236)

The analogy between thoughts and sentences holds for fine,
as well as gross, structures.

> There is not a conjunction or a preposition, and hardly
> an adverbial phrase, syntactic form, or inflection of voice,
> in human speech, that does not express some shading or
> other of relation which we at some moment actually feel
> to exist between the larger objects of our thought. . . .
> We ought to say a feeling of *and*, a feeling of *if*, a
> feeling of *but*, and a feeling of *by*, quite as readily as we
> say a feeling of *blue* or a feeling of *cold*. (1:238)

Although William James implies here that consciousness is
structured like a language, he is not arguing that it is exclusively verbal. His point is that all mental activity is a stream:
a continuous flow with resting-places. Contrary to those psychologists who maintain that all thought is linguistic, William
James argues forcefully that the stream takes many forms: "Let
A be some experience from which a number of thinkers start.
Let *Z* be the practical conclusion rationally inferrible from it.
One gets to the conclusion by one line, another by another;
one follows a course of English, another of German, verbal
imagery. With one, visual images predominate; with another,
tactile" (1:260). Thus it makes sense to talk of a perceptual
stream.

William James proposes the stream in its various forms as a correction to the associationist notion of a "chain" of distinct, atomistic ideas. He explicitly disagrees with Alexander Bain's associationist insistence that "'the stream of thought is not a continuous current, but a series of distinct ideas'" (1:237–38). Instead, James calls for "the re-instatement of the vague to its proper place in our mental life" (1:246). And he argues that, not only are most of our thoughts vague "*feelings* of *tendency*," but even the resting-places, the nouns, are continuous with the surrounding "water of consciousness" (1:246). "Every definite image in the mind is steeped and dyed in the free water that flows round it. With it goes the sense of its relations, near and remote, the dying echo of whence it came to us, the dawning sense of whither it is to lead" (1:246).

Strether's first viewing of Maria Gostrey's apartment illustrates this liquid continuity of the perceptual stream: "It was the innermost nook of the shrine—as brown as a pirate's cave. In the brownness were glints of gold; patches of purple were in the gloom; objects all that caught, through the muslin, with their high rarity, the light of the low windows. Nothing was clear about them but that they were precious" (21:119–20). What he sees is a continuous whole. There are resting-places (the glints, the patches, the objects), but they are immersed in their surroundings (in the brownness, the gloom, the light).

Rather than a series of discrete ideas, one replacing another, William James describes a changing flow in which perceptions "melt" into one another "like dissolving views" (1:269). Gazing at the crowded scene in Gloriani's garden, Strether finds that "he had just made out, in the now full picture, something and somebody else; another impression had been superimposed" (21:220). There is no break. Idea does not succeed idea, but impression flows over impression.

Often, Henry James uses atmosphere and light to convey this sense of a full, fluid perceptual context (a technique that, as Chapters 3 and 4 will show, is important to his landscapes as well): "The night was hot and heavy and the single lamp sufficient; the great flare of the lighted city, rising high, spending itself afar, played up from the Boulevard and, through the vague vista of the successive rooms, brought objects into view and added to their dignity" (22:210).

As this passage hints, the stream of perception flows toward discrimination. At Maria Gostrey's, Strether begins to discriminate certain objects more clearly, and eventually he is "bent, with neared glasses, over a group of articles on a small stand" (21:123). He still sees a continuous whole, yet his seeing now entails analysis. Associationism describes the mind as passively receiving simple units of sensation which build up into complex structures. For both William and Henry James, the procedure is exactly reversed. William James explains that "the 'simple impression' of Hume, the 'simple idea' of Locke are both abstractions, never realized in experience. Experience, from the very first, presents us with concreted objects, vaguely continuous with the rest of the world which envelops them in space and time, and potentially divisible into inward elements and parts. These objects we break asunder and reunite" (1:61).

William James says explicitly that this discrimination is perceptual. He argues that even conceptual divisions can be ultimately traced to perceptual discriminations. Yet those critics who recognize how the movement, the continuity, the "vagueness," to use William James's word, in Henry's sentences are the very terms of analysis and discrimination, do not realize that these complexities are often perceptual. Instead, these attributes are ascribed to a rational intellect that is seeking to *control* the raw material of perception. Because it is assumed that perception is simple and atomistic, what the eye sees and what the mind knows are regarded as qualitatively different. Stowell, for example, who uses the image of the *tabula rasa* to characterize perception, argues that "consciousness" synthesizes discrete, raw precepts into an active, processive gestalt.[4] The idea that, for James, perceptions are the crude bits of material between which "thinking" discerns relations rests on the critical failure to recognize that both Jamesian thought and Jamesian perception are streams. "This way of taking things belongs with the philosophy that looks at the *data* of sense as something earth-born and servile, and the 'relating of them together' as something spiritual and free" (2:675).

By arguing that Strether's discriminations are perceptual, not "spiritual," I am not, of course, denying that James's characters have nonvisual thoughts.[5] My point is that, for James, perception is as finely tuned and complex as other mental processes. Indeed, perception often entails mental actions, like problem solving, that are assumed to be the work of "higher" intellectual faculties. To use William James's terms, Strether comes to his conclusion, he gets to Z, through a kind of visual thinking.

In order to understand how one could perform such sophisticated operations perceptually, we need to recognize the distinction William James makes between pure sensation and perception. For James, sensation's "function is that of mere *acquaintance* with a fact. Perception's function, on the other hand, is knowledge *about* a fact; and this knowledge admits of numberless degrees of complication" (2:652). Even the sensations of infancy are not completely raw and unprocessed, but are instead structured by the body. After the first days of life, we perceive, rather than sense; in adulthood, "*pure sensation*" is "*an abstraction*" (2:653). Thus, while he may seem to be seeing Maria Gostrey's apartment with what Ruskin calls "the innocence of the eye," that is, seeing "an arrangement of patches of different colours variously shaded" (15:27), Strether's perceptions are *not* innocent, as phrases like "brown as a pirate's cave" make clear. Comparatives point to a past, to experience.

Strether's perceptual flow is structured like a language precisely in that it is semiotic—what constitutes the visual stream is a chain of signifiers. Strether's visual images signify metonymically, contextually, historically; they are saturated with associations, associations that are themselves not only visual but also verbal, aural, and the like.

Taking as his starting point Derrida's "Il n'y a pas de perception," John Carlos Rowe argues that "in the novels and tales, interpretations may masquerade as visual impressions, but there are no impressions that are not always already involved in complex semantic, social, and historical determinations. . . . There is no perception, no impression in the ocular or present sense possible in James's epistemology." What I am arguing is that "the textuality of 'consciousness' " that Rowe describes so accurately here ("complex semantic, social, and historical determinations") is traceable in the "ocular" perception that he denies. By de-emphasizing the physical, Rowe disembodies the Jamesian eye and I.[6]

The materiality of Jamesian perception is illustrated by the way that the visual provides the "language" of analysis in Maria Gostrey's apartment. What Strether finds in the sight of the down-to-earth entresol is a corrective to his puzzlement about Chad and Paris. This clarifying recognition takes the form of the rather blurry brown picture described above. Strether's picture of Maria's apartment is both the statement of, and the solution to, his predicament. He works the problem out visually. Strether sees Maria's apartment as, like Paris, and like Chad, at once confusing and alluring. It is a dark maze in which he can discriminate only the glint of precious objects. That is the problem. But the entresol is neither Paris nor Chad's troisième. It is Maria's home. And therein lies the solution. For Strether soon sees that "after a full look at his hostess he knew none the less what most concerned him. The circle in which they stood together was warm with life, and every question between them would live there as nowhere else" (21:120).

The sight of the apartment's owner transforms the scene into a full, warm circle—still intricate, but now accessible. Maria's presence in the midst of the maze brings the scene to order. That the entresol is her home explains both her and it. Strether's growing ability to distinguish the bibelots is not simply emblematic. Instead, his perception here is actually the next step in his understanding. What he literally sees in Maria's apartment both allows him to understand Maria herself (her taste, her expertise, her knowledge) and permits him to analyze Chad. The narrator tells us that Strether first "glanced once more at a bibelot or two, and everything sent him back" (back, that is, to the bibelots in Chad's apartment) (21:123). Maria's furnishings are a visual reminder of Chad's, and her homier setting becomes a means to understanding the owner of the "mystic troisième." Rather than describing how Strether uses some higher faculty to synthesize crude perceptual building blocks into a complex whole, James shows the stream of Strether's perception as a process that moves toward discrimination and analysis.

Recognizing how the critical dichotomy between primitive perception and complex thought distorts the psychology of James's perceivers is important because of a related, more serious, distortion that underlies much James criticism. This is the mistaken opposition between True Reality, which is "seen" by the mind, and False Appearance, which is seen by the eye.[7] As his characters' reliance upon perception makes clear, James sets up no such antithesis. Reality can be known only through its appearance; characters know through seeing. Because both perception and its objects are complex, appearances can easily be oversimplified or misunderstood; nonetheless, what the eye sees and what the mind knows are not in opposition. At Gloriani's garden party, Strether sees the great artist as "a fine worn handsome face, a face that was like an open letter in a foreign tongue. With his genius in his eyes, his manners on his lips, his long career behind him and his honours and rewards all round, the great artist, in the course of a single sustained look and a few words of delight at receiving him, affected our friend as a dazzling prodigy of type" (21:196). The fact that Strether has not fully learned the visual language in which Gloriani's self is written does not mean that appearances lie. His perception, informed by past viewings of Gloriani's work, is an intricate mix of the known and the unknown. As George Eliot argues in *Adam Bede*, "Nature has her language, and she is not unveracious; but we don't know all the intricacies of her syntax just yet, and in a hasty reading we may happen to extract the very opposite of her real meaning."[8] And Strether recognizes that Gloriani's eyes *are* "the penetrating radiance, as the communication of the illustrious spirit itself" (21:197).

Like James's, Eliot's environments are complexly social. Yet the differences between the ways the two writers describe their characters' visual relations with those social environments are telling. Comparing Eliot's and James's practices illustrates the analytic nature of the Jamesian perceptual stream. Midway through *Middlemarch*, after a long night of watching, Dorothea awakens to the realization that her crisis is shared by three others (Will, Rosamund, and Lydgate) and is brought to a question.

> "What should I do—how should I act now, this very day, if I could clutch my own pain, and compel it to silence, and think of those three?"
> It had taken long for her to come to that question, and there was light piercing into the room. She opened her curtains, and looked out towards the bit of road that lay in view, with fields beyond outside the entrance-gates. On the road there was man with a bundle on his back

and a woman carrying her baby; in the field she could see figures moving—perhaps the shepherd with his dog. Far off in the bending sky was the pearly light; and she felt the largeness of the world and the manifold wakings of men to labour and endurance. She was part of that involuntary, palpitating life, and could neither look out on it from her luxurious shelter as a mere spectator, nor hide her eyes in selfish complaining.

What she would resolve to do that day did not yet seem quite clear, but something that she could achieve stirred her as with an approaching murmur which would soon gather distinctness.[9]

Clearly what Dorothea sees in this famous scene is determined in part by what she thinks and knows. As many Eliot critics have observed, she has often looked out this window before, but now, for the first time, she notices human figures in the scene. Similarly, James marks Strether's growing knowledge by having him return to the various Parisian apartments. But despite the selective activity implicit in Dorothea's focus on the human figures, her perception remains largely static. She has had her realization before she looks out the window, and she turns back into the room with no new knowledge. What she sees reflects, but does not affect, her thoughts. The three people that she sees are emphatically *not* Will, Rosamund, and Lydgate because the scene is a symbol for her life, rather than a part of it. The man bearing a bundle, and the woman a child, the shepherd and the dog, are emblems for "labor and endurance." There is no *visual* interaction here between Dorothea and the world "outside the entrance-gates."[10]

Strether perceives more actively and processively. What he sees does not merely reflect a question arrived at or even a question answered. Instead, the answering of the question, the problem-solving process, takes place *in* the stream of Strether's perceptions. As we have already observed, his early analytic picture of Maria Gostrey's apartment aids him in understanding Chad. Perceiving Maria's entresol for the second time, he confronts the problem of Maria herself. Strether distinguishes the fact that Marie de Vionnet has been there, and he works his way to a realization of the guilty association between the two women. "He was sure within a minute that something had happened; it was so in the air of the rich little room that he had scarcely to name his thought. Softly lighted, the whole colour of the place, with its vague values, was in cool fusion—an effect that made the visitor stand for a little agaze. It was as if in doing so now he had felt a recent presence" (22:295).

The room is no longer intricate and varied. Strether now sees it as uniformly lit and open to easy understanding. He solves the problem of how to judge Maria Gostrey by looking at her apartment and seeing in the "cool fusion" and "vague values" her tie to the other woman. The two phrases are pointed allusions to Marie de Vionnet. In descriptions of her apartment, colors are repeatedly referred to as "cool," and the painterly term "values" is used explicitly. And, of course, the complicity of the two women has effected a guilty sort of fusion between them, just as Maria's values have been, at best, "vague"—she has silently consented to Strether's deception.

Strether does not know all of these things before he arrives. His understanding comes *as* he composes his visual picture of the entresol. Indeed, his visual conclusion is so vivid that verbal expression becomes secondary: "He had scarcely to name his thought." The moment of perception is a moment of engagement with the problems of life. Strether's role as a representative Jamesian perceiver marks him not as a passionless intellect who stands apart and waits for impressions, but as an active, interested self who survives by perceiving.

Strether survives in his world by seeing what he needs to see. His perceptual pictures are always self-interested—even when they seem self-sacrificing. For example, he constructs a series of pictures of Marie de Vionnet that portray a lady in mild, romantic distress and thus in need of noble, yet limited, "saving." These pictures permit Strether to become safely, restrictedly, involved with her. Strether's need to think of himself as noble does not prevent him from acting nobly. His selfish eye is not the mark of a villain because it is not an organ peculiar to Strether. He does not rationally decide to see as he does—indeed, he is usually not aware of the way his interests direct his perceptions. Instead, Strether's visual pictures are structured by the very conditions of seeing. To discover that what the Jamesian eye sees is always in the interest of the Jamesian "I," is not to uncover secret evil in James's protagonists. In the Notes to *The Sense of the Past*, James describes Ralph Pendrel as "all selfishly" asking another for help and then goes on to say: "Immense and interesting to show him as profiting by her assistance without his being thereby mean or abject or heartless" (26:328, 338). Our understanding of Strether's self-interested seeing needs to be equally "immense."

We need also to understand that Strether cannot completely determine what he sees. His self-interested activity is immediately limited by what Hocks calls the " 'outside' determinations" of his environment. Although from the very start he selects and arranges in the act of seeing, Strether's visual surroundings are often designed by others.[11] For example, Chad offers Strether a series of charming, nonthreatening visual substitutes for himself. When he does arrange for Strether to see him, Chad repeatedly manages to stand above the seated older man. The surprise appearance at the theatre is an obvious example of Chad's manipulations of the conditions of perception. This staged show ensures that Strether will see, not "Chad," the wayward boy whom he expects to chastise, but the handsome Europeanized man who towers over him.

As Strether's inability to recognize Chad indicates, past interactions with his environment also restrict what he sees. William James calls "inveterate . . . our habit of not attending to sensations as subjective facts, but simply using them as stepping-stones to pass over to the recognition of realities whose presence they reveal" (1:225). Our perceptual pasts, in other words, provide us with useful shortcuts: "Our hemispheres, in particular, are given us in order that records of our private past experience may co-operate in the reaction" (2:747). Early in the novel, Strether finds himself in the Luxembourg Gardens because the "current of association" has floated him there (21:90). Knowing only that he will "recognise as soon as see it the best place of all" to read his American letters, Strether, without consciously realizing it, is guided by visual clues along *Chad's* route through Paris (21:78–79). Similarly, Strether's perception of Madame de Vionnet during his last visit to the Rue de Bellechasse is one in which records of all of his past viewings of Marie and her apartment "co-operate."[12]

> The associations of the place, all felt again; the gleam here and there, in the subdued light, of glass and gilt and parquet, with the quietness of her own note as the centre . . . he was sure in a moment that, whatever he should find he had come for, it wouldn't be for an impression that had previously failed him. . . . She might intend what she would, but this was beyond anything she could intend, with things from far back—tyrannies of history, facts of type, values, as the painters said, of expression—all working for her and giving her the supreme chance . . . to be natural and simple. (22:275–76)

Unsettled by the day in the country, Strether reassures himself that he will see nothing new. He is unwittingly correct. Although Strether does not achieve his hoped-for "natural and simple" picture of Marie, the "mixed" perception of her which ends this meeting points to an earlier sight (22:284). He recognizes "the refined disguised suppressed passion" (22:131) that he detected in her face on his last visit, sees again the restless, desperate woman he saw in the country, perceives that Marie is afraid for her life.

Such perceptual "records" are often strong enough to take the form of mental images or preperceptions. "When, however, sensorial attention is at its height, it is impossible to tell how much of the percept comes from without and how much from within; but if we find that the *preparation* we make for it always partly consists of the creation of an imaginary duplicate of the object in the mind, which shall stand ready to receive the outward impression as if in a matrix, that will be quite enough to establish the point in dispute" (1:415). Perhaps the clearest illustration of Strether's tendency to preperceive comes when he ascends the stairs of Chad's apartment for his final visit. As he climbs, Strether begins to think about Chad's evening. He starts with nonvisual supposings, but *before* he reaches Chad's door, Strether literally sees before him an image of the apartment.

> He had been for a week intensely away, away to a distance and alone; but he was more back than ever, and the attitude in which Strether had surprised him was something more than a return—it was clearly a conscious surrender. He had arrived but an hour before, from London, from Lucerne, from Homburg, from no matter where— though the visitor's fancy, on the staircase, liked to fill it out; and after a bath, a talk with Baptiste and a supper of light cold clever French things, which one could see the remains of there in the circle of the lamp, pretty and ultra-Parisian, he had come into the air again for a smoke, was occupied at the moment of Strether's approach in what might have been called taking up his life afresh. (22:305–6)

William James states, "Each present brain-state is a record in which the eye of Omniscience might read all the foregone history of its owner" (1:228). We can read Strether's visual history in the components of this preperceptive image: the past sight of Little Bilham smoking on the balcony; the breakfast that resulted, a "repast of so wise a savour" (21:113); his midnight exposure to the "soft circle" of Chad's "single lamp" (22:209–10); his early perceptions of the circle, "warm with life" (21:120) in Maria's entresol. But Chad restlessly refuses to hold still and conform to Strether's idealized image of him as the perfect Parisian. He guides Strether out of the apartment, deliberately removing himself from the setting that has, in the past, fostered just such images. Chad comes down from the superior heights of the "mystic troisième," and his low nature becomes visually obvious: "Chad had thrown back his light coat and thrust each of his thumbs into an armhole of his waistcoat; in which position his fingers played up and down" (22:316). Once in the street, Chad turns into a caricature of the American Advertising Man.[13]

Strether's anticipatory image on the stairs is unusual. Generally, rather than describing Strether's preperceptions as such, James shows how these visual preparations order present sights. As William James explains:

> The *preperception*, as Mr. Lewes calls it, is half of the perception of the looked-for thing.
>
> It is for this reason that men have no eyes but for those aspects of things which they have already been taught to discern. . . . In short, *the only things which we commonly see are those which we preperceive*, and the only things which we preperceive are those which have been labelled for us, and the labels stamped into our mind. If we lost our stock of labels we should be intellectually lost in the midst of the world. (1:419–20)[14]

The past intrudes upon and organizes the present. For example, Strether's first perception of Marie de Vionnet is structured by Woollett sights and labels: "She was dressed in black, but in black that struck him as light and transparent; she was exceedingly fair, and, though she was as markedly slim, her face had a roundness, with eyes far apart and a little strange. Her smile was natural and dim; her hat not extravagant; he had only perhaps a sense of the clink, beneath her fine black sleeves, of more gold bracelets and bangles than he had ever seen a lady wear" (21:210). Madame de Vionnet's black strikes Strether as light and transparent because Mrs. Newsome's is dark and opaque. Similarly, he perceives her hat as, in a negation of Woollett expectations, "not extravagant." That she wears "more gold bracelets and bangles than he has ever seen a lady wear" implies that, while her jewelry is not that of a Woollett lady, Strether cannot categorize her as "not a lady." All of these discriminations take place in the very act of perception.

William James argues that the associationist notion that we hold the separate "ideas" of "*m*" and "*n*" next to one another in our minds and compare them, that the past is simply a point of objective comparison for the present, is mistaken. Instead, we experience "*n*" in light of our past experiences of "*m*." The "*pure* idea of '*n*' is *never in the mind at all*, when '*m*' has once gone before; and . . . the feeling [of] '*n-different-from-m*' is itself an absolutely unique pulse of thought" (1:472–73). When, in the opening scene of the novel, Strether sees the Chester city wall, he does not contrast this present perception with his original sight of the wall. Instead, what he sees is "enriched" by what he saw: "Too deep almost for words was the delight of these things to Strether; yet as deeply mixed with it were certain images of his inward picture" (21:16). In the garden of the Tuileries, his past perceptions lead him to see, not a blank space, but an "irremediable void" where the palace once stood (21:79).

Despite the past's hold over what is seen, the present does appear to have some power. Part of Strether's perceptual freedom comes from his capacity to learn. For example, he learns to modify his Woollett category of "lady" in the face of Marie de Vionnet's appearance. And Strether acquires new labels as well. He begins by being unable to pick the *femmes du monde* out of the crowd at Gloriani's, but learns to recognize Madame de Vionnet at Chad's as belonging to that category. Yet Strether lacks the ability to entirely free himself of old perceptual categories, as this very perception of Marie as a *femme du monde* graphically illustrates.[15] Because his past training will not permit Strether to admire Marie's sexuality, he focuses on her shoulder, arms, neck, and head. His comparison of this perception to that of "a goddess still partly engaged in a morning cloud, or . . . a sea-nymph waist-high in the summer surge" confirms the past's control over what Strether sees (21:270).[16]

A more limited, and yet potentially more liberating, source of perceptual freedom lies in Strether's power of attention, an activity William James defines as "the taking possession by the mind, in clear and vivid form, of one out of what seem several simultaneously possible objects or trains of thought" (1:381–82). When Strether returns to Paris and sees yellow books in a store window, he is inevitably affected by the fact that he saw them thirty years ago. The associative mechanism causes his past perceptions to condition his present ones, but, at the same time, Strether's present perception does not replicate his past ones. Free will is located in the perceptual nexus between past and present. In his youth the books seemed to him symbols of his plans for greatness. Now they appear as signs of the loss of that youth, an effect that he intensifies by focusing on the glass that shields them. Strether *attends*: He forbids himself the purchase of any books, ensuring that he will see them with "hungry gazes through clear plates behind which lemon-coloured volumes were as fresh as fruit on the tree" (21:86). James makes the perceiver's share in perception explicit by showing Strether seeing, not books, but books behind a window. Strether makes sure that he perceives the pleasures of Paris through a clear, but clearly present, barrier.[17] His ability to freely select may be circumscribed, but it exists, and he acts upon it. Strether's characteristic turning away, his directing his vision toward safe objects (in moments of stress he repeatedly turns to look at his American letters or watch), are examples of the limited but powerful faculty that William James calls "mental spontaneity." "*My experience is what I agree to attend to.* Only those items which I *notice* shape my mind—without selective interest, experience is an utter chaos. Interest alone gives accent and emphasis, light and shade, background and foreground—intelligible perspective, in a word" (1:380–81).

This spontaneous activity is a constant in Henry James's descriptions of visual perception. When Strether needs to be able to think of Marie de Vionnet as a romantic lady in distress, he creates a picture of her apartment that suits his purposes. Chad has prepared for this scene by praising Marie, carrying Strether off to the visit, and leaving the two alone. But Strether's own participation is evident in the description of the apartment. He works hard at what he sees: "he found himself making out, as a background of the occupant"; "he guessed"; "his attention took them all tenderly into account"; "he quite made up his mind" (21:244–45). Although he conjectures that the apartment "went further back" (21:244), Strether persists in seeing it as belonging to the Romantic period so that he can select and arrange its details into a High Romantic picture: "He would have answered for it at the end of a quarter of an hour that some of the glass cases contained swords and epaulettes of ancient colonels and generals; medals and orders once pinned over hearts that had long since ceased to beat; snuff-boxes bestowed on ministers and envoys; copies of works presented with inscriptions, by authors now classic" (21:246).

He can even discern the inscriptions! Once Strether can see Marie de Vionnet ensconced in a heroic, historic setting, he can believe that she is a lady in mild distress and he, a self-sacrificing knight. The picture he creates permits him to become involved with her in a noble, safe way. Of course, Marie has helped to make sure that this picture was available to Strether. Reversing Chad's visual ploy of standing above Strether, she even seats herself on the apartment's one anomalously modern chair so that he can see her in the lowly position of supplicant. "Then it was that he saw how she had decidedly come all the way; and there accompanied it an extraordinary sense of her raising from somewhere below him her beautiful suppliant eyes. He might have been perched at his door-step or at his window and she standing in the road" (21:248). As Strether's analogies indicate, Marie's pose helps him to direct his associations. The scene becomes familiar—an illustration to a melodramatic romance.[18]

This interaction between arranged environment and attentive eye is explicit in the picture of Marie de Vionnet that she and Strether create together at Notre-Dame. Immediately following Strether's declaration to Little Bilham that if Chad gives up Marie de Vionnet, he "ought to be ashamed of himself" (21:286), Strether's visit to the church is described. His betrayal of Woollett values, together with his visual "habit . . . of watching a fellow visitant" and seeing his or her posture as evidence of the penitence—and absolution—that he himself half-consciously desires, leads him to attend to the "lurking" female figure (22:6, 8). Bringing to bear an array of artistic associations, he perceives the figure he has selected to perceive as a heroine. When Marie turns to face Strether, she offers him the materials with which to complete the picture he has prepared himself to see:

> He confessed the extent of his feeling, though she left the object vague; and he was struck with the tact, the taste of her vagueness, which simply took for granted in him a sense of beautiful things. *He was conscious of how much it was affected*, this sense, by something subdued and discreet in *the way she had arranged herself for her special object* and her morning walk—*he believed her to have come*

on foot; the way her slightly thicker veil was drawn—a mere touch, but everything; the *composed* gravity of her dress, in which, here and there, a dull wine-colour seemed to gleam faintly through black; the *charming discretion* of her small compact head; *the quiet note,* as she sat, of her folded, grey-gloved hands. (22:8–9; italics mine)

They manage the same picture again in Mrs. Pocock's salon— "She looked much as she had looked to him that morning at Nôtre Dame; he noted in fact the suggestive sameness of her discreet and delicate dress"—although this is certainly not what Sarah sees (22:93). A "discreet and delicate" portrait of Marie de Vionnet neither fits her preperceptions nor serves her purposes.

Attention's ability to overcome the past's mechanical structuring of the present is also active in the workings of memory. By remembering, Strether prevents his past from automatically determining his future. Such a statement seems paradoxical only because of confused or casual notions about how memory works. William James explains:

> Memory proper . . . *is the knowledge of an event, or fact,* of which meantime we have not been thinking, *with the additional consciousness that we have thought or experienced it before.* . . . And it is an assumption made by many writers that the revival of an image is all that is needed to constitute the memory of the original occurrence. But such a revival is obviously not a *memory,* whatever else it may be; it is simply a duplicate, a second event, having absolutely no connection with the first event except that it happens to resemble it. . . . No memory is involved in the mere fact of recurrence. (1:610–11)

Strether's recognition of the Lambinet in the French countryside is not the longed-for revival of a past image: "He never found himself wishing that the wheel of time would turn it up again, just as he had seen it in the maroon-coloured, skylighted inner shrine of Tremont Street" (22:246). The notion that Hocks describes as central to both William James's pluralism and Henry James's later manner—"The same returns not, save to bring the different"—obtains here.[19] Strether remembers, rather than repeats, the past. "It would be a different thing, however, to see the remembered mixture resolved back into its elements—to assist at the restoration to nature of the whole faraway hour: the dusty day in Boston, the background of the Fitchburg Depot, of the maroon-coloured sanctum, the special-green vision, the ridiculous price, the poplars, the willows, the rushes, the river, the sunny silvery sky, the shady woody horizon" (22:246). Rather than reexperiencing his Boston perceptions on the train, Strether analyzes the past into its essential "elements" and watches for the material with which to recompose a new version of the scene. His choice of a stop is precisely that: a choice. The visual memory of Tremont Street and the visual opportunity of his environs allow him to create his own French picture—"weather, air, light, colour, and his mood all favouring" (22:246).

In Rowe's words, Strether "recognizes the specular image of his own historical subjectivity";[20] he is the producer, as well as the product, of that historical self. The active, reciprocal interaction between organism and environment that William James describes exists in and over time; the world Strether visually sculpts for himself is a world in four dimensions. What Strether's perceptual freedom, limited though it may be, allows is James's narrative flexibility. The story of *The Ambassadors*, James tells us in his Preface, is the story of how a man comes to make a speech in a garden. Yet, rather than a plodding chronology of the events that, one by one, led to this event, we have *The Ambassadors*, the narrative of a character who *reflects on*, as well as reflects, his past.[21] Functionalism allows James to place his protagonist in an environment and within a personal history without locking either his character or his text into a literary determinism. "The business of my tale and the march of my action, not to say the precious moral of everything, is just my demonstration of this process of vision," James states (21:vi). Studying precisely what it is that Strether literally sees, examining the way the process of vision is enacted in the stream of visual perception, reveals how actively Strether engages in the struggle to shape his environment and self.

Notes

1. For example, Marianna Torgovnick's *The Visual Arts, Pictorialism, and the Novel: James, Lawrence, and Woolf* (Princeton: Princeton University Press, 1985), an anatomy of literary uses of the visual arts, uses *The Ambassadors* as its primary example of "perceptual" pictorialism.

2. Ruth Bernard Yeazell, *Language and Knowledge in the Late Novels of Henry James* (Chicago: University of Chicago Press, 1976), 17. Yeazell goes on to suggest that such intellectual control is "more precarious—and more hard-won—than might at first appear" (18).

3. Although William James is widely acknowledged to be the originator of this phrase, J. Gill Holland has claimed priority for G. H. Lewes in "George Henry Lewes and 'Stream of Consciousness': The First Use of the Term in English," *South Atlantic Review* 51 (January 1986): 31–39.

4. H. Peter Stowell, *Literary Impressionism, James and Chekhov* (Athens: University of Georgia Press, 1980), 24–25. See also Judith Ryan, "The Vanishing Subject: Empirical Psychology and the Novel," *PMLA* 95 (1980), who describes Henry James's characters as making mental connections between their "often disparate and discontinuous sensory perceptions" (859). Ryan fails to recognize that the image of the stream characterizes the way sensations are actually *experienced*, not simply the way the mind perceives itself.

5. For an excellent discussion of the intricacies of Jamesian thought and language, see Yeazell's *Language and Knowledge*. Jamesian perception is, however, for Yeazell, simple: "Perception of sensuous correspondences is direct and immediate, but the world of the late novels does not allow of such easy connections among its parts" (41).

6. John Carlos Rowe, *The Theoretical Dimensions of Henry James* (Madison: University of Wisconsin Press, 1984), 194, 202. What

Rowe and Derrida term "perception" is closer to what William James calls "sensation."

7. See, for example, Daniel J. Schneider's chapter, "The Eye, Appearances, and Acting," 96–116, in *The Crystal Cage: Adventures of the Imagination in the Fiction of Henry James* (Lawrence: The Regents Press of Kansas, 1978). Schneider describes well James's characters' abilities to manipulate appearances, but mistakenly concludes that what the eye sees "is contrasted with the natural and with the invisible, the real, the *ding in sich*" (98). Both Richard A. Hocks's book, *Henry James and Pragmatistic Thought* (Chapel Hill: University of North Carolina Press, 1974), and N. I. Bailey's short article, "Pragmatism in *The Ambassadors*," *Dalhousie Review* 53 (1973): 143–48, demonstrate that such formulations describe neither Henry's nor William's thought.

8. George Eliot, *Adam Bede*, Cabinet Edition, 2 vols. (Edinburgh & London: William Blackwood, 1878–80), 1:229.

9. George Eliot, *Middlemarch*, Cabinet Edition, 3 vols. (Edinburgh & London: William Blackwood, 1878–80), 3:392.

10. For an opposing reading, see Hugh Witemeyer, *George Eliot and the Visual Arts* (New Haven: Yale University Press, 1979), who argues that this landscape "makes possible a creative interaction between her mind and the world outside it" (154).

11. Hocks, *Henry James*, 177. Torgovnick also notes a number of Strether's visual arrangements, as well as others' attempts to arrange sights for him (*The Visual Arts*, 174–78).

12. See Hocks's comments on the "recognition scene" in the country: "Strether actively and radically meets the discovery; he enters into a reciprocal relation with it, grafting meaning while receiving in kind; he empties every possible insight about himself, his previous assumptions, the thoughts of the two lovers in having to deal with *him*, and even the imagined responses of those back at Paris, into it" (*Henry James*, 63).

13. On Chad and advertising, see William Greenslade, "The Power of Advertising: Chad Newsome and the Meaning of Paris in *The Ambassadors*," *ELH* 49 (Spring 1982): 99–122.

14. Yeazell, *Language and Knowledge*, makes a similar point, without recourse to William James: "Language creates the conditions under which perception is possible" (75).

15. In contrast, see Paul B. Armstrong, *The Challenge of Bewilderment: Understanding and Representation in James, Conrad, and Ford* (Ith-

aca: Cornell University Press, 1987), who describes Strether's "bewilderment" at Chad's transformation as happily freeing him from old Woollett "categories" and "terms" (66–70). Bailey more accurately stresses the past's power.

16. This editing has been noted by a number of critics. Strether's most vivid perceptions of women throughout the novel tend to be focused on the upper halves of their bodies.

17. James makes the cultural context of this perception explicit in *The American Scene*, where the plate glass, which makes the books unobtainable objects of desire, appears as the agent and emblem of consumerism. See Chapter 3 of this volume.

18. See Viola Hopkins Winner, *Henry James and the Visual Arts* (Charlottesville: University of Virginia Press, 1970), 1 ff., on how James's own visual perceptions of the world were affected by his early viewings of illustrated books.

19. Hocks, *Henry James*, 86–89.

20. Rowe, *The Theoretical Dimensions*, 198.

21. As Hocks says in another context, "There is the same basic difference between [Henry] James's various 'principles' and his *Prefaces* in which they are presumed to reside, as between 'Lambert Strether journeys to Europe on behalf of Mrs. Newsome' and the opening chapters of *The Ambassadors*" (*Henry James*, 54).

CHAPTER 2

The Opening Door

Seeing the Self in The Golden Bowl

LAMBERT STRETHER'S active, interested, functional seeing provides a paradigm for James's other perceivers. Maggie Verver sees as Strether does. Having used Strether's sights as explanatory examples of functionalism, I want to reverse my emphasis and show how understanding the functional nature of Jamesian perception allows us to read *The Golden Bowl*.

Like Strether, Maggie attempts to remember, not repeat, the past. While William James assents to the associationists' powerful argument that *"time- and space-relations . . . are* impressed from without," he goes on to demonstrate that "the images impressed upon our memory by the outer stimuli are not restricted to the mere time- and space-relations, in which they originally came, but revive in various manners" (2:1229). Associationism does not recognize the infinite variety of ways in which "experiences befall in a mind gifted with memory, expectation, and the possibility of feeling doubt, curiosity, belief, and denial" (2:1230). Maggie's perceptions reveal how the environmental order of experience impresses its pattern on her, yet they also show her ability to visually select a history and thus a self. Like Strether's, Maggie's functional perceptions evidence both association and activity. Rather than passively following the associative paths of the past, Maggie, by seeing interestedly, attentively, and selectively, attempts to repattern her present. William James's attention to those psychological events that conventionally remain unnoticed because unnamed helps to explain the pace and the path of Henry James's narrative. His characters achieve visual knowledge, not by being bombarded with a sequence of discrete sensations, but through a temporally complex process that includes anticipation and absence, indirection and delay. *The Golden Bowl* subtly traces the looping path whereby Maggie comes to know her self and her social environment even as she helps to shape them.

In achieving visual perception, Maggie comes to self-consciousness. The word "achieving" is crucial here. In *The Golden Bowl*, the process of becoming self-conscious is anxiously focused upon by the character herself. William James's criticism, throughout *The Principles of Psychology*, of what he calls "the Psychologist's Fallacy" helps to clarify Maggie's situation. He argues that psychologists mistakenly assume "*that the mental state studied must be conscious of itself as the psychologist is conscious of it*" (1:195). This fallacy results from a failure to recognize an important distinction. "What the thought sees is only its own object; what the psychologist sees is the thought's object, plus the thought itself, plus possibly all the rest of the world" (1:196). The condition in which thought is "conscious of itself as the psychologist is" is not ordinary consciousness; it is the condition toward which Maggie struggles: self-consciousness.

This emphasis on self-consciousness marks a major divergence between *The Ambassadors* and *The Golden Bowl*.[1] Maggie's and Strether's perceptual situations vary because of a difference between what might be called the temporal *directions* of knowledge in the two novels. While Strether manages to hold off knowledge of Marie and Chad's adultery until nearly the end of his novel, Maggie knows quite early on that Amerigo and Charlotte are intimate. Maggie does not refuse knowledge, but she does try to avoid its consequences. She struggles not only to achieve, but also to resist, self-consciousness. James illustrates her attempt and its failure by showing the logical working out of what Maggie knows in what she sees. If Strether's pictures reveal the history of the present, Maggie's visual images display the present realization of the past.

Henry James's emphasis in *The Golden Bowl* on a *visible* self-consciousness highlights the fact that knowledge is itself a factor in the social environment. Awareness of what is known is not merely a private event. Maggie's role as creator as well as creature of her environment is made manifest by the way her knowledge and self-consciousness become visible forces both for herself and for others.

Self-consciousness in *The Golden Bowl* is profoundly social because the Jamesian self is socially defined. Indeed, a complete description of the visual construction of social selves in the novel would entail analysis of all of the characters' perceptions—and make this far too long a chapter. Thus, while I do discuss both Amerigo and Charlotte as perceivers at several points, my focus is on what Maggie sees. That the self Maggie comes to consciousness of by seeing is a profoundly social one is reflected in James's original title for the novel, *The Marriages*. Rowe points out that "not only is marriage the primal social institution, but it is also a familiar Jamesian metaphor for the relation of consciousness to the world."[2] But in arguing that marriage should consist of an "intersubjective relation" (204) rather than "social forms" (209), and in condemning "Maggie's determination to save the marriages rather than the people involved" (209), Rowe assumes the existence of natural selves, separate from "imposed" (210) and "artificial" (211) social roles.[3] There are no such "people" in James's world. As Allen demonstrates, "Struggle as self . . . involves a protection and con-servation of social forms."[4] Maggie's visual perceptions of her environment help her to recognize how living with others defines and limits her.[5] By locating the Princess's self-recog-nition socially, James demonstrates that our private identities are publicly constituted; as William James maintains, "The innermost of the empirical selves of a man is a Self of the *social* sort" (1:301).[6]

Despite William James's generic "man," Jamesian social selves are, as Allen's analysis in *A Woman's Place in the Novels of Henry James* shows, deeply and conventionally gendered. Yet the Jamesian dance of seeing and being seen breaks with con-vention in that it does not inevitably partner a male spectator with a female object. Even Strether's picture of Marie de Vion-net as a lady in distress is at least partly staged by Marie herself, and Chad is equally the object and the orchestrator of Strether's perceptions. The lovers in some sense make spectacles of them-selves for Strether. Nonetheless, it is his language of images that finally identifies them: "It's how you see me, it's how you see me . . . and it's as I *am* and as I must take myself," Marie de Vionnet cries to Strether (22:285). In *The Golden Bowl*, James anatomizes this defining power of the gaze, but by displaying the female as perceiver, he further deconstructs the gendered opposition between seer and seen.[7]

The process of Maggie's growth to consciousness of this social self takes place not only in the progress of her external perceptions, but also in her stream of mental images.[8] In his essay on *The Golden Bowl*, Gabriel Pearson maintains that "a marked fact about James's fiction is the way in which his concentration on scenic representation precludes any real op-eration of his facts, objects and backgrounds on the formation of his characters' fates. . . . Their [the facts', objects', and back-grounds'] tendency is to disappear into the interiority of met-aphor, or purely mental action" (307).[9] External and internal worlds *do* resemble one another in *The Golden Bowl*, yet they do so not in their mutual unreality, but in their shared *material* reality.[10] Maggie's mental images are vivid perceptual events, which, taken together, constitute a language of visual images, a network of psychological phenomena. In their repeated but reluctant surfacing, Maggie's mental images display her resisting movement toward self-consciousness.

Nonetheless, Pearson's claim does identify a slippage that pervades James's narratives. As Yeazell says, "However we may try to keep the minds of the narrator and his characters properly distinct, the language of the late novels themselves continually defeats us."[11] This stylistic "fluidity" (12) can make it difficult to distinguish between mental image and narrative metaphor, a difficulty heightened by that fact that, as Strether's example shows, Jamesian visual perceptions are never innocent of verbal associations, and by the way that visual metaphors inform James's narrative language. One current of this complex crossing of the visual and the verbal is charted in Rowe's deconstruction of "literary impressionism," which uncovers the impression as the site of writing, "the divided present and rhetorical catachresis in which language finds its own origins, even as it preserves this secret beneath the gaze of the eye and the voice of the I."[12] Attention to Maggie's perceptual images reveals a countering representational pressure: an inclination toward the visual so strong that occasionally what begins as a metaphor ends as a (represented) perception.[13]

"It is the Prince who opens the door to half our light upon Maggie, just as it is she who opens it to half our light upon himself; the rest of our impression, in either case, coming straight from the very motion with which that act is performed," James declares in the novel's Preface (23:viii). He is describing the novel's structural division into two parts, but the motion of opening, rather than the completed act, pervades *The Golden Bowl*'s narrative on other levels as well. Maggie's movement to self-consciousness is portrayed through the ongoing interaction of her streaming perceptions and her fluctuating environment, and through the play of present consciousness over the associations of the past. In opening doors, Maggie perceives how her present identity is a function of, and a functioning agent in, her social environment and her personal history.

The Mistress of the Table

The opening of Maggie's self-consciousness is visibly displayed in the scene where she paces the floor at Portland Place, "watching by his fireside for her husband's return from an absence" at Matcham.[14] As when Strether actually sees the "irremediable void" that the removal of the Tuileries palace has created, Maggie sees incompleteness, a picture of something missing. Similarly, when Adam disappears for American City at the end of the novel, Maggie *sees* his absence: "the great grey space on which, as on the room still more, the shadow of dusk had fallen" (24:366). Rather than disappearing as if he had never existed, Adam leaves a void. However, Maggie's perception of Amerigo's absence differs from the other two examples because what she sees on the Matcham day is saturated with anticipation. She experiences what William James calls "feelings of tendency" (1:240). When we are told to " 'Wait!' 'Hark!' 'Look!' " or when "we try to recall a forgotten name," we focus on no new "object" of perception or sensation and, therefore, according to associationist theory, experience nothing. William James argues that, on the contrary, such states are "attitudes of expectancy.... A sense of the direction from which an impression is about to come, although no positive impression is yet there" (1:243). We become conscious of a gap, "a gap that is intensely active" (1:243). Such states have been ignored, William James argues, because of a basic weakness in psychological vocabulary. What he shows is that "namelessness is compatible with existence. There are innumerable consciousnesses of emptiness, no one of which taken in itself has a name, but all different from each other. The ordinary way is to assume that they are all emptinesses of consciousness, and so the same state. But the feeling of an absence is *toto coelo* other than the absence of a feeling: it is an intense feeling" (1:243–44).

The gap that Maggie sees and the desire that prompts its sight lead to the perception that culminates this scene: Amerigo's appearance as he opens the door. Maggie reads her social situation, and with it her self, in this perception of her husband taking his place at their fireside.

What is striking about visual perception in *The Golden Bowl* is the intricate process involved in attaining this self-conscious sight. Well before Amerigo returns and opens the door, we become aware that Maggie is intensely aware of her thoughts, her actions, even of her clothes. Yet, at the same time, trying to keep calm so that she will be able to act naturally when the Prince arrives, Maggie struggles to avoid self-consciousness. This ambivalence is expressed through Maggie's perception of her own physical appearance. She finds that making herself "quite inordinately fresh and quite positively smart, . . . had probably added, while she waited and waited, to that very tension of spirit in which she was afterwards to find the image of her having crouched" (24:12). Her appearance both bolsters her sense of self and makes her apprehensive. "[She] had refused herself the weak indulgence of walking up and down, though the act of doing so, she knew, would make her feel, on the polished floor, with the rustle and the 'hang,' still more beautifully bedecked. The difficulty was that it would also make her feel herself still more sharply in a state; which was exactly what she proposed not to do" (24:12–13).

Maggie's awareness and avoidance of her "bedecked" condition are an awareness and avoidance of her self. Early in his discussion of the "*constituents of the Self*," William James points out that after the body, which is "the innermost part of *the material Self*. . . . The clothes come next. The old saying that the human person is composed of three parts—soul, body and clothes—is more than a joke. We so appropriate our clothes and identify ourselves with them that there are few of us who, if asked to choose between having a beautiful body clad in raiment perpetually shabby and unclean, and having an ugly and blemished form always spotlessly attired, would not hesitate a moment before making a decisive reply" (1:280).

Maggie's dress identifies her as the beautiful, grand lady-wife. This scene replays an earlier rainy March afternoon when Amerigo waits in vain for Maggie to appear at his fireside as "mistress of the table" (23:294). She now wants to reclaim this identity, both in her own eyes and Amerigo's. And yet she does not want to reclaim it, for she does not want to acknowledge that she has ever lost or left this role. Her attitude toward her external appearance makes this contradiction clear: the resplendent reflection of herself in the polished floor attracts and appalls her, for it shows her both in the mistress-of-the-table role and, nervously overdressed and tensely pacing, *taking up* that role.[15] In *The Ambassadors* a woman is also seen reflected in the polished floor of her salon. The difference between these two superficially similar perceptions illustrates *The Golden Bowl*'s emphasis on self-consciousness: Strether sees two Marie de Vionnets; Maggie sees herself. Maggie cannot simply become as she once was—Amerigo's confident, loving wife—because that Maggie never reflected upon herself in that role: she simply acted it. Now Maggie wants to be reassured that she is filling her place; she wants to know herself in it. Maggie desires the impossible: knowledge without knowledge's effect, self-consciousness as self-knowledge without self-consciousness as awkward self-awareness.

Maggie's solution to her dilemma—how to feel prepared to meet Amerigo without feeling that she has prepared—is to focus not on the reflection of her bedecked, pacing self, but to sit still and look down at her dress. "The only drops of her anxiety had been when her thought strayed complacently, with her eyes, to the front of her gown, which was in a manner a refuge, a beguilement, especially when she was able to fix it long enough to wonder if it would at last really satisfy Charlotte" (24:13).

The difference between looking down at her dress and watching a full-length reflection of herself is the difference between asking "What does she think of the way I look?" and "What does he think of what I know?" But, despite her efforts at complacency, the questions that Maggie asks herself build up "accumulations of the unanswered" (24:14). Maggie's attempt to deal with this mass of unknown quantities introduces the door image and with it an extraordinary mix of self-consciousness, consciousness, and repression:

> They were *there*, these accumulations; they were like a roomful of confused objects, never as yet "sorted," which for some time now she had been passing and re-passing, along the corridor of her life. She passed it when she could without opening the door; then, on occasion, she turned the key to throw in a fresh contribution. So it was that she had been getting things out of the way. They rejoined the rest of the confusion; it was as if they found their place, by some instinct of affinity, in the heap. They knew in short where to go, and when she at present by a mental act once more pushed the door open she had practically a sense of method and experience. What she should never know about Charlotte's thought—she tossed *that* in. It would find itself in company, and she might at last have been standing there long enough to see it fall into its corner. The sight moreover would doubtless have made her stare, had her attention been more free—the sight of the mass of vain things, congruous, incongruous, that awaited every addition. It made her in fact, with a vague gasp, turn away, and what had further determined

this was the final sharp extinction of the inward scene
by the outward. The quite different door had opened and
her husband was there. (24:14–15)

Although the room seems to begin as the narrator's metaphor
("like a roomful"), by the end of the passage it is clearly Maggie's mental image, her "inward scene." What William James
describes as the ability to think visually holds true for internal
as well as external sights. Maggie's mental image is at once an
analysis and an avoidance of the external perception that finally
replaces it. She thinks the problem through by watching her
mental image.

On the one hand, the image offers a relatively straightforward explanation for Maggie's storing the Charlotte questions
away. She does not repress the questions; she asks them of
herself. Maggie then consciously takes the "accumulations of
the unanswered" and closes the door on them. Again this is
not a case of the simple repression of threatening material. The
answers to her questions about Charlotte are not known to be
dangerous; they are gaps in knowledge, contentless "answers"
that she puts away.[16]

However, as William James's discussion of "the feeling of
absence" makes clear, a gap is not the same as a blank. Further,
the issue of repression is hard to avoid because the back room
of Maggie's psyche sounds, particularly to the post-Freudian
ear, like the unconscious.[17] Although William James saw no
need to postulate an "unconscious," he documents repeatedly
that we direct our conscious attention away from much that
we already know. Certain potential objects of attention "simply *go out*; and to keep the mind upon anything related to them
requires such incessantly renewed effort that the most resolute
Will ere long gives out and lets its thoughts follow the more
stimulating solicitations after it has withstood them for what
length of time it can. There are topics known to every man

from which he shies like a frightened horse, and which to get a glimpse of is to shun" (1:398).[18]

Interest not only directs attention, it guides inattention as well. Maggie's inability, or refusal, to focus visually on the Charlotte questions bespeaks both her desire not to see them and her interest in another, more "stimulating," sight. Why is Maggie's attention not "free"? A clue lies in her action as she disposes of the "things," pacing up and down, "passing and re-passing, along the corridor of her life." Maggie enacts mentally the physical pacing that she has earlier forbidden herself. This displacement is an attempt to overcome anxiety. Worrying about what Charlotte thinks is a distraction, a way of screening the fact that Maggie *is* dressed, *is* waiting, *is* tense. Maggie gets rid of the Charlotte questions, not only because they are unanswerable, but also because they cannot hide the problem of Amerigo. Her attention is not "free"; the screen does not work.

Yet while the Charlotte questions are secondary, they do, in that they are questions of appearance, mirror Maggie's primary concern: the effect that her conscious reappearance as mistress of the table will have. Closed doors both make space for, and ward off, the image of which Maggie has become self-conscious—her reappearance as the mistress—and the necessary complement to this image—the reappearance of the master: "The quite different door had opened and her husband was there."

Like Strether, Maggie attends. She turns to the sight that serves her interests most fully. Amerigo's appearance—returned from Matcham, framed by the door that he has just opened, regarding her—figures the public nature of her problem. His position fixes hers and, together with his gaze of recognition, reveals their interdependent social identities ("her husband"). As William James explains, the connection between our selves and the images that others hold of us is intensely real.

> Those images of me in the minds of other men are, it is
> true, things outside of me, whose changes I perceive just
> as I perceive any other outward change. But the pride
> and shame which I feel are not concerned merely with
> *those* changes. I feel as if something else had changed too,
> when I perceive my image in your mind to have changed
> for the worse, something in me to which that image
> belongs, and which a moment ago I felt inside of me,
> big and strong and lusty, but now weak, contracted, and
> collapsed. (1:306)

Living in the world of others, we acquire social selves. These
identities are neither superficial nor trivial. We care about and
incorporate them into our persons. And, as William James's
example illustrates, this dependency on others, a dependency
inherent in social existence, makes identity precarious.

Intimacy only increases identity's instability. "The most peculiar social self which one is apt to have is in the mind of
the person one is in love with. The good or bad fortunes of
this self cause the most intense elation and dejection—unrea-
sonable enough as measured by every other standard than that
of the organic feeling of the individual. To his own consciousness he *is* not, so long as this particular social self fails
to get recognition, and when it is recognized his contentment
passes all bounds" (1:282).

Henry James shows the dark side of this intimate recognition.[19] Amerigo "had come back, had followed her from the
other house, *visibly* uncertain—this was written in the face he
for the first minute showed her" (24:15). Despite the fact that
Amerigo is uncertain about and embarrassed before Maggie,
he is "a master of her fate" (24:21) because she values his image
of her. In facing Amerigo, Maggie faces the unanswered questions, uncertainties, and risks of social self-consciousness. She
must contend with others' reactions to her and to what she
knows. In this sense, outer door is much like inner door—
Amerigo resurrects the buried question of Maggie's appear-

ance.[20] In another sense, however, the door that Amerigo opens is "quite different" from Maggie's inner door because it opens a relation between consciousnesses rather than within consciousness. Amerigo's visual presence opens the door between mental state and social situation, self and other, knowledge and action.

The Red Mark of Conviction

Maggie's opening social self-consciousness is a mixed blessing. What she sees reveals how fixed she is by the way past events have structured her social situation. Maggie begins to visually "make out" the marks of arrangement in the physical structures of domesticity that surround her and, in turn, to discern the visible signs of this growing knowledge in the blushes that suffuse the cheeks of her social circle. Perhaps the most frightening instance of Maggie's social and temporal imprisonment comes as she and Amerigo return from an Eaton Square dinner party. Amerigo struggles to control the situation, but Maggie refuses to give in to her husband. However, as they stop in front of Portland Place, Maggie realizes that she has, in fact, lost the struggle:

> She alighted the next instant with a slight sense of defeat; her husband, to let her out, had passed before her and, a little in advance, awaited her on the edge of the low terrace, a step high, that preceded their open entrance, on either side of which one of their servants stood. The sense of a life tremendously ordered and fixed rose before her, and there was something in Amerigo's very face, while his eyes again met her own through the dusky lamplight, that was like a conscious reminder of it. (24:66–67)

The footman may have literally opened the carriage door for Maggie, but Amerigo controls her passage through it: He "let her out." The carriage door opens only to visually display to Maggie the social arrangement in which Amerigo is trying to contain her. Maggie's motion is restricted to a short walk between conjugal carriage and conjugal manor. The open door leads not to freedom, but to another door, where Maggie's husband stands above her, guarded on either side by servants, waiting to hand her into his domain and close the door after her. Like Chad, the Prince assumes a superior position in order to intimidate visually. Maggie sees in Amerigo's eyes that he will try to use the role of wife as a way of fixing her, of limiting her freedom.

In reaction to this and other manifestations of her imprisonment, Maggie turns to the idea of motion. "Maggie went, she went—she felt herself going"; "Oh she was going, she was going"; "And since I wanted to 'go' I'm certainly going" (24:33; 24:51; 24:69). Both Maggie's entrapment and her run for freedom have become standard components of most readings of *The Golden Bowl*. What has remained unnoticed, however, is that this need for motion is not simply a wish for personal freedom. Maggie tries to transform the very nature of social identity, both for herself and for others. She wants to change from narrowly labeled roles to flexible relations—altering self and environment simultaneously. Further, Maggie desires to free the quartet *temporally*. "She had been able to marry without breaking, as she liked to put it, with her past" (24:5); now Maggie realizes the necessity of this break. Trying to shatter the link of consistency between past and present, she appears in unexpected places, behaves in unprecedented ways, says unlikely things, attempts to "*dis*arrange" (24:45).[21] Maybe, somehow, her inconsistencies will allow the four to stay together in an eternal, free present of multiple, not mutually exclusive, relations. "Daughter" and "wife" will no longer contradict each other.[22]

Yet Maggie's desire for inconsistency rests upon a consistent history that she inevitably seeks to preserve. Her break for freedom must not (cannot) entail a total rupture with the past. Maggie's work at disarrangement, then, is limited not only by Charlotte's and Amerigo's attempts to hold her in the old arrangement, but also by her own inclinations toward *rear-rangement*. What Maggie sees shows her "mental spontaneity," but William James's qualification bears repeating: "Even though there be a mental spontaneity, it can certainly not create ideas or summon them *ex abrupto*. Its power is limited to *selecting* amongst those which the associative machinery has already introduced or tends to introduce" (1:559). Even as she runs for fluidity and freedom, Maggie's new present is restricted to a repatterning of the past.

We can trace Maggie's mixed inclinations in the perceptions that follow her chance stop in the Bloomsbury antique store. She has attained the knowledge she has sought since that Matcham weekend. Her suspicion that Charlotte and the Prince have been "intimate" (24:161) has been matched with visual proof: the golden bowl itself, and, at the bowl's breaking, Amerigo's flushed face. A blush is, by its nature, both a mark of personal knowledge and a profoundly social, and socialized, reaction.[23] Yet Maggie's reaction to this display of a shared spousal intelligence is surprising: "Left with her husband Maggie however for the time said nothing; she only felt on the spot a strong, sharp wish not to see his face again till he should have a minute to arrange it. . . . Maggie knew as she turned away from him that she didn't want his pain; what she wanted was her own simple certainty—not the red mark of conviction flaming there in his beauty" (24:181–82).

James illustrates the futility of Maggie's wish for certainty without conviction by showing the public nature of her growing knowledge. Traceable in Amerigo's blush is a social history. The discovery of the bowl created "the bright red spot, red as some monstrous ruby, that burned in either of her cheeks" (24:152), that marked Maggie's awareness of Charlotte and Amerigo's intimacy. The breaking of the bowl left both Fanny and the Princess "flushed" (24:179). Maggie recognizes that Amerigo's "red mark of conviction" also recalls his appearance on the Matcham evening, when he first displayed the possibility of her knowledge (24:181). Maggie's is both a visual and a visible education. By knowing, she alters her environment; in William James's figure, she sculpts her world.

The social results of Maggie's "certainty" are made clear by James's pun on "conviction." Maggie cannot be certain that the Prince is guilty of intimacy without convicting him for adultery, both in her eyes and in his. Her desire for "bandaged eyes" (24:182) comes too late. She seems to have escaped her old arrangement only to be rearranged in a social order. She will be the Wronged Wife; Amerigo, the Convicted Adulterer. As Seltzer's Foucauldian analysis of *The Golden Bowl* makes clear, what seems to be "Maggie's" power actually "inheres in the structure of relations among characters" (70). Thus, "every exercise of power is inevitably doubly binding" (70).[24] The bandage marks *Maggie* as a condemned prisoner. In convicting Amerigo, she has convicted herself. Their present and their future will be locked into a permanent arrangement of reaction to their past.

Cats and Cages

Despite these blushes of shared knowledge, Maggie continues to use the strategies of silence, concealment, and waiting, in a desperate attempt to forestall the future, to suspend the quartet in an eternal present where the events of the past will have no determining effect.[25] But such strategies for the social survival of the self cannot merely be directed outwards because, as James shows throughout *The Golden Bowl*, self and society are not separately constituted and therefore not in simple opposition. Maggie's mental images reveal that patient delaying is a tactic being used within consciousness as well as between consciousnesses. Just as she tries to keep her knowledge from others, so she tries to keep it from herself. Yet Maggie's convictions surface again and again in her mental images.

Perhaps the most remarked, and least understood, image in *The Golden Bowl* is Maggie's picture of Charlotte as a great cat. Usually treated as a brilliant individual example of a Jamesian metaphor, the picture is, in fact, part of a semiotic network of associated images of cats, cages, and prisoners that Maggie literally sees, mental pictures that eventually affect her external perceptions of Charlotte. This language of visual images is aptly described by William James's characterization of the stream of associations: "Trains of imagery and consideration follow each other through our thinking, the restless flight of one idea before the next, the transitions our minds make between things wide as the poles asunder, transitions which at first sight startle us by their abruptness, but which, when scrutinized closely, often reveal intermediating links of perfect naturalness and propriety" (1:519). Focusing her attention on particular images in this stream, scrutinizing her pictures of Charlotte, Maggie moves toward self-consciousness.

The connection between Charlotte and cages is first introduced at the end of Book 5, Chapter 1, when Maggie is wondering how Amerigo has managed not to tell Charlotte that he knows Maggie is aware of the intimacy. Maggie is convinced that she and Amerigo have been at one in keeping Charlotte in the dark, and, consequently, she pities the other woman:

> Even the conviction that Charlotte was but awaiting some chance really to test her trouble upon her lover's wife left Maggie's sense meanwhile open as to the sight of gilt wires and bruised wings, the spacious but suspended cage, the home of eternal unrest, of pacings, beatings, shakings all so vain, into which the baffled consciousness helplessly resolved itself. The cage was the

deluded condition, and Maggie, as having known delusion—rather!—understood the nature of cages. She walked
round Charlotte's—cautiously and in a very wide circle;
and when inevitably they had to communicate she felt
herself comparatively outside and on the breast of nature:
she saw her companion's face as that of a prisoner looking through bars. So it was that through bars, bars richly
gilt but firmly though discreetly planted, Charlotte
finally struck her as making a grim attempt; from which
at first the Princess drew back as instinctively as if the
door of the cage had suddenly been opened from within.
(24:229–30)

Despite her belief that Charlotte is waiting to attack, Maggie
sees the other woman compassionately. The Princess imagines
her stepmother suffering as she herself has—baffled, ignorant,
locked in the cage of "delusion"—and mourns her imprisonment. The position that Maggie visualizes for herself, "outside,
on the breast of nature," and her imaging of Charlotte first as
bird and then, by implication, as beast, imply that Maggie
desires a state of nature, free from the prisonlike structures of
civilization. Maggie's mental image is an expression of empathy and identification: two women reflecting one another
across prison bars.

It is an image that eerily echoes Charlotte Perkins Gilman's
1892 story, "The Yellow Wallpaper." Like the narrator in
Gilman's story, Maggie comes to an understanding of her self
and her social environment by watching such pictures. But the
differences between the two narratives are instructive. Restricted and repressed by others, Gilman's protagonist with-
draws into an inner hallucinatory world. James's heroine's
mental images are, on the other hand, survival tools. What
Maggie sees brings her to an understanding both of the dangers
of her social environment—the threat that others present to
her—and of her own social power.

These dangers account for the enmity displayed in Maggie's
seemingly empathetic images.[26] The Princess's "conviction"

of Charlotte's assault necessarily entails condemnation as well as certainty. Maggie has convicted Charlotte of adultery, and her mental image expresses her thought. After all, both the pitiful, caged Charlotte and the cruel cage are images created by Maggie. If Maggie starts off seeing only a bird cage, her final drawing back from the vision hints at a coming transformation. Maggie's position is only "comparatively" natural; recognizing that society's cages confine the self, she nonetheless "instinctively" realizes that prison bars are also a source of protection.

In the next chapter, after Maggie has fled the smoking room where she has been tempted to reveal her knowledge and disrupt the card game, she sees the cage again. Maggie realizes that Charlotte has followed her, and this change in arrangement strikes Maggie as "a breaking of bars" (24:239). The appearance of Charlotte, "launched and erect" (24:238), reveals that "the splendid shining supple creature was out of the cage, was at large; and the question now almost grotesquely rose of whether she mightn't by some art, just where she was and before she could go further, be hemmed in and secured" (24:239). Bird changes to beast; empathy through the bars becomes the anxious desire to secure and strengthen those barriers. The negative feelings that were hinted at in the first image of the cage here become fully manifest. At the same time, Maggie's positive feelings for Charlotte have not disappeared. Splendid creature and prison-like cage or dangerous predator and protective bars? Beauty or beast? Disarrangement or rearrangement? Maggie's mixed feelings about her entire social situation are imaged in her pictures of Charlotte.

These pictures are challenged by Charlotte herself, who, as her appearances before Amerigo throughout the novel illustrate, is powerful in the art of self-presentation.[27] Outside on the terrace, the two women engage in a battle for visual mastery. Maggie finds herself "perceiving that the thing she feared had already taken place. Charlotte, extending her search, appeared now to define herself vaguely in the distance. . . . Yes, Charlotte had seen she was watching her from afar, and had stopped now to put her further attention to the test. Her face was fixed on her, through the night; she was the creature who had escaped by force from her cage" (24:241). Maggie recognizes her image of the other as a dangerous cat, but also faces reluctantly ("vaguely"; "dimly discerned" [24:241]) Charlotte's ability to "define herself." Charlotte's deliberate appearance threatens not only Maggie's image of her, but also the Princess's own social identity. "Her face was fixed on her"—as Charlotte presents herself to be seen, she fixes Maggie before her. Locked into a "mutual look," Maggie "felt herself absolutely take from her visitor something that the latter threw upon her" (24:241–42).

What Maggie seems to take from Charlotte is a new self. "Maggie had kept the shawl she had taken out with her, and, clutching it tight in her nervousness, drew it round her as if huddling in it for shelter, covering herself with it for humility. She looked out as from under an improvised hood—the sole headgear of some poor woman at somebody's proud door; she waited even like the poor woman" (24:247).

Although this pose expresses Maggie's sincere admiration for and fear of Charlotte, it is only a pose. The final sentence quoted above continues, "She met her friend's eyes with recognitions she couldn't suppress" (24:247). Maggie's double consciousness, her knowledge and its concealment, is visibly revealed: the fearful beggar with the knowing eyes.[28] Charlotte's power on the terrace rests on Maggie's need to conceal her own strength. The beast that Maggie fears is, like John Marcher's, a metaphor for herself. She has tried to "get away, in the outer darkness, from that provocation of opportunity which had assaulted her, within on her sofa, as a beast might have leaped at her throat" (24:235). Maggie sees Charlotte as

a dangerous cat, not because she thinks Charlotte will phys-
ically or verbally attack her, but because she fears how she
herself will behave with her stepmother. If the Princess does
not keep her conviction of Charlotte and Amerigo's guilt to
herself, Charlotte will outwardly reflect and express that conviction. Maggie, faced with this concrete manifestation of her
own knowledge, will be forced into full self-consciousness of
her hostility toward her stepmother and rival. Charlotte, having listened to Maggie, will speak to Adam. The quartet will
become rearranged in antagonism. What the earlier image of
two women reflecting one another across prison bars displays
is that individual identity is neither private nor free. Embedded
in their social environment, James's characters are defined by
their reactions to one another.

So it is only when Maggie is safely away from her stepmother in the next chapter that she allows herself to see the
impress of her strength on Charlotte. After Adam threatens to
ship off to America, an image fills Maggie's field of vision:
"Ah then it was that the cup of her conviction, full to the
brim, overflowed at a touch! *There* was his idea, the clearness
of which for an instant almost dazzled her. It was a blur of
light in the midst of which she saw Charlotte like some object
marked by contrast in blackness, saw her waver in the field of
vision, saw her removed, transported, doomed" (24:271).

Although this picture of a ghostlike, doomed Charlotte contrasts pointedly with that of her as a cat, Maggie does not
reflect on the identity of the two Charlottes until several days
later. Then she realizes what the images that she has already
seen, already created, mean:

> A few days of this accordingly had wrought a change in
> that apprehension of the instant beatitude of triumph—
> of triumph magnanimous and serene—with which the
> upshot of the night-scene on the terrace had condemned
> our young woman to make terms. She had had, as we

know, her vision of the gilt bars bent, of the door of the cage forced open from within and the creature imprisoned roaming at large—a movement on the creature's part, that was to have even for the short interval its impressive beauty, but of which the limit, and in yet another direction, had loomed straight into view during her last talk under the great trees with her father. It was when she saw his wife's face ruefully attached to the quarter to which in the course of their session he had so significantly addressed his own—it was then that Maggie could watch for its turning pale, it was then she seemed to know what she had meant by thinking of her, in the shadow of his most ominous reference, as 'doomed.' (24:283)

Seeing Charlotte look where Adam has—directly at Maggie—Maggie becomes aware that she already knows her stepmother's fate.[29] Juxtaposing her two images of Charlotte, she recognizes that the latter is the limit of the former. Free for only a "short interval," the beast now has a new cage—the cage of causal connection, the prison of time. Charlotte of the past (Amerigo's lover, a dangerous and beautiful beast) determines Charlotte of the future (Adam's unfaithful wife, a transported and pitiful convict). One image is the logical working out of the implications of the other.[30]

Although Maggie is said to become aware of these things through a "change in apprehension," she has been seeing these images all along. The very first picture of the cat figures the self-knowledge that Maggie tries to avoid. Her seeming ambivalence toward Charlotte was actually an attempt to poise their relationship in a fluid timeless present where she could both admire and control her friend and rival. The inexorable logic of Maggie's images points to her failure. The beauty and threat of Charlotte free call for (in fact, seem to call up) the horror and the relief of Charlotte captive. The only new "apprehension" is Charlotte's: she is the convict who must be transported.

Maggie's strategy of waiting, then, works subtly against her acknowledged intent. Ostensibly, she is trying to disarrange: to contain knowledge, prevent reaction, and forestall the future. Yet her period of waiting and silence provides time for mental images of her knowledge to appear and reappear. Gradually but inexorably, they lead Maggie toward self-consciousness of her inevitable conviction of Charlotte and, by implication, of her final rearrangement of the quartet. Maggie's waiting does not stop time, but instead allows its forward passage, permits the links between knowledge and its effects to strengthen themselves. Analyzing Maggie's visual images shows how James's narrative can trace the temporally convoluted paths of his characters' consciousnesses (the pauses, the delays, the backtracking), at the same time that it unfolds the chronological development of their fates. James's narrative tactics are played out in Maggie's visual strategies.

Convicts and Cells

What Maggie has learned—and tried not to learn—visually culminates in the final perceptions of the novel. Actively struggling to perceive new images of a free future, Maggie sees instead historical sights. Associations with the past inform her present vision; cages and other enclosures, blushes, and pacing prisoners proliferate. For example, on Adam and Charlotte's last day in Europe, Amerigo's external appearance reveals to Maggie his trapped condition:

> The Prince was in his "own" room, where he often sat now alone; half a dozen open newspapers, the *Figaro* notably, as well as the *Times*, were scattered about him; but with a cigar in his teeth and a visible cloud on his brow he appeared actually to be engaged in walking to and fro. Never yet on thus approaching him—for she had done it of late, under one necessity or another, several times— had a particular impression so greeted her; supremely

> strong, for some reason, as he turned quickly round on
> her entrance. The reason was partly the look in his face—
> a suffusion like the flush of fever, which brought back
> to her Fanny Assingham's charge, recently uttered under
> that roof, of her "thinking" too impenetrably. . . . His
> way of looking at her on occasion seemed a perception
> of the presence not of one idea, but of fifty, variously
> prepared for uses with which he somehow must reckon.
> (24:337–38)

The past echoes visually in this scene. Amerigo's inability to sit still as man of the house contrasts perceptibly with Adam's earlier assumption of this posture.[31] Seeing her husband pacing, Maggie realizes that both his role and his restlessness are domestically constituted. The sight of his face prompts her to recall Fanny's remark, but she does not mention, perhaps does not realize, that her association is visual: Amerigo's flushed face. Just as "the red mark of conviction flaming there in his beauty" (24:182) mirrored Maggie's red-faced consciousness of Amerigo's guilt after the breaking of the golden bowl, the Prince's face is here marked by a partial reflection of Maggie's feverish ideas. Facing one another in marriage, the Prince and Princess display the conditions of social existence.

> Even after she had stepped into his prison under her
> pretext, while her eyes took in his face and then embraced
> the four walls that enclosed his restlessness, she recog-
> nised the virtual identity of his condition with that aspect
> of Charlotte's situation for which, early in the summer
> and in all the amplitude of a great residence, she had
> found with so little seeking the similitude of the locked
> cage. He struck her as caged, the man who couldn't now
> without an instant effect on her sensibility give an in-
> stinctive push to the door she hadn't completely closed
> behind her. (24:338)

Like Charlotte, the Prince has been caged by Maggie's knowledge. Long ago Amerigo opened the door between Maggie's consciousness and the world. Now the scene is fully and frighteningly reversed. Maggie has opened the door between her and the Prince: "She had begun, a year ago, by asking herself how she could make him think more of her; but what was it after all he was thinking now?" (24:339). The Princess's position, blocking and guarding the door, reveals the dark side of social self-consciousness. Maggie holds the key to Amerigo's social self; what she knows will determine how he will know himself.

Maggie's power becomes fully apparent when Amerigo says that he is going "correct" Charlotte by telling her that he lied to her:

> " 'Correct' her?" . . . "Aren't you rather forgetting who she is?" After which, while he quite stared for it, as it was the very first clear majesty he had known her to use, she flung down her book and raised a warning hand. "The carriage. Come!"
>
> The "Come!" had matched for lucid firmness the rest of her speech, and when they were below in the hall there was a "Go!" for him, through the open doors and between the ranged servants, that matched even that. He received Royalty, bareheaded, therefore, in the persons of Mr. and Mrs. Verver, as it alighted on the pavement, and Maggie was at the threshold to welcome it to her house. (24:356)

In asking her second question, Maggie directs Amerigo to the quartet's history. Charlotte is Amerigo's former companion and lover; Maggie's former friend and rival; Adam's wife. In the Jamesian world of relational identities, to abruptly admonish Charlotte would be to devalue all who have been so intimately related to her. Even if the quartet is now two couples, Maggie needs to preserve the importance of each of its members.

Yet, while defending Charlotte's place in the group, Maggie calls into question Amerigo's. Correcting Amerigo for daring to suggest that he might correct Charlotte, Maggie issues orders, sending the bareheaded Prince outside like a humble servant while she waits above him at the threshold to welcome the guests to "*her* house" (italics mine). Maggie's desire to "go" has been transformed into the "Go!" of her command to Amerigo. Earlier Maggie felt herself "ordered and fixed" (24:66) as she walked toward the spectacle of their servants ranged on either side of the house door where her husband stood above her. That door seemed to open onto a prison of social arrangement. Now, instead of wife walking from carriage to house, husband walks from house to carriage. The open door connects the elements of Amerigo's domestic situation: house, servants, wife, father-in-law, and stepmother-in-law. His brief walk outside, circling within these social structures, merely replicates his prisoner's pace inside. Amerigo's path leads back to Maggie's house.

Within that domestic prison, Charlotte and Amerigo have assigned roles. Charlotte's performance as the visual center of attention—"throned . . . between her hostess and her host . . . the harmony wasn't less sustained for being superficial" (24:358)—is actually a display of the powers behind the throne, of Maggie and Adam's deeper harmony. Agreeing that Charlotte is "great," father and daughter "stood together over it quite gratefully, each recording to the other's eyes that it was firm under their feet" (24:364). They stand on her majesty. When the Prince, continuing to play the servant, offers his father-in-law a plate of petits fours, the sugary, miniature nature of the quartet's accord is made explicit.

Even Adam and Charlotte's start for America does not bring the "clear liberation" from the prison of the past that Maggie had hoped for (24:342). "Maggie's going out to the balcony again to follow with her eyes her father's departure. The carriage was out of sight—it had taken her too long solemnly to reascend, and she looked a while only at the great grey space on which, as on the room still more, the shadow of dusk had fallen" (24:366). There is no such thing as a fresh start. The Prince and Princess return; Maggie re-ascends. As William James's example of how we hear a thunderclap reveals, the reverberating silence of expectation that surrounds Maggie is not a neutral backdrop for the scene that follows: "Into the awareness of the thunder itself the awareness of the previous silence creeps and continues; for what we hear when the thunder crashes is not thunder *pure*, but thunder-breaking-upon-silence-and-contrasting-with-it" (1:234). The past creeps in visually as well, as Maggie sees the dusk connecting the grey void without and the twilit emptiness by her side: "She stood in the cool twilight and took in all about her where it lurked her reason for what she had done" (24:367). The "reason" for her father's absence is the figure who will fill the domestic gap, a sight "foredoomed" by past perceptions to "remarkable salience"—Amerigo.

Maggie's *"potential social self"* (1:300), to use William James's phrase, depends upon another. Using himself as an example, William James explains that even apparently independent behavior is actually socially determined:

> I am always inwardly strengthened in my course and steeled against the loss of my actual social self by the thought of other and better *possible* social judges than those whose verdict goes against me now. . . . The emotion that beckons me on is indubitably the pursuit of an ideal social self, of a self that is at least *worthy* of approving recognition by the highest *possible* judging companion, if such a companion there be. This self is the true, the intimate, the ultimate, the permanent Me which I seek. (1:300–301)

William James goes on to argue that, finally, this judge is God. However (Christian readings of *The Golden Bowl* to the contrary), there is no divine tribunal for Henry James's protagonist. Maggie's "highest *possible* judging companion" is Amerigo. But the sight of Amerigo is not simply that of a loving husband, it is the sight of that husband looking at his wife. Amerigo comes to Maggie with a visible consciousness of past events; what is worse, he appears with a knowledge of her consciousness of past events. "It kept him before her therefore, taking in—or trying to—what she so wonderfully gave. He tried, too clearly, to please her—to meet her in her own way; but with the result only that, close to her, her face kept before him, his hands holding her shoulders, his whole act enclosing her, he presently echoed: ' "See"? I see nothing but *you*.' And the truth of it had with this force after a moment so strangely lighted his eyes that as for pity and dread of them she buried her own in his breast" (24:368–69).

If "not to be known is Maggie's triumph," as Bayley maintains, she is a double failure: known to her husband and herself.[32] Maggie has become Amerigo's "highest possible judging companion." Trying to please her, he is reduced to an echo. Rather than, as Holland argues, "setting the past behind him," husband traps wife before the visible evidence of their conjugal history.[33] The novel ends with them locked in an embrace, in the "steel hoop of intimacy" that results from social self-consciousness.[34] Maggie's knowledge has convicted them both, and her earlier longing for a blinding bandage is satisfied at last as she hides her eyes so as neither to see or be seen. Maggie and Amerigo's future will be an inexorable working out of the actions and knowledge of the past.

The door to Maggie's self-consciousness is permanently open, but it offers no escape from an unrelenting self-awareness. She cannot forget what she knows, and, even if she could, she cannot escape its effect on her world. Her convictions are visibly before her.

Lambert Strether is both the creature, and the creator, of his environment. Attention, actively directed by interest, allows

Strether to select his perceptions. What Strether sees shows how his past informs and structures, rather than mechanically determines, his present. Maggie Verver, perceptually similar to Strether, sees and is seen in a very different psychological and physical environment. As both her mental images and social perceptions make clear, James gives us in Maggie a character profoundly conscious of her self and, thus, of others. In doing so, he demonstrates how both self-consciousness and society impinge upon present freedom. It is precisely because Maggie is so powerful a creator of her environment that she is so much its creature. She lives in a world that mirrors her. Despite Maggie's undeniable activity as a deeply interested perceiver of the present, she ends by looking back.

Notes

1. See Richard A. Hocks, *Henry James and Pragmatistic Thought* (Chapel Hill: University of North Carolina Press, 1974), 188–96, for a description of other ways in which critics have distinguished *The Ambassadors* from both *The Golden Bowl* and *The Wings of the Dove*.

2. John Carlos Rowe, *Henry Adams and Henry James: The Emergence of a Modern Consciousness* (Ithaca: Cornell University Press, 1976), 203.

3. Similar assumptions underlie Leo Bersani's argument that Maggie manages, through love, to remove Amerigo from society and history. See "The Jamesian Lie," in *A Future for Astyanax: Character and Desire in Literature* (Boston: Little, Brown, 1976), 126–55.

4. Elizabeth Allen, *A Woman's Place in the Novels of Henry James* (New York: St. Martin's Press, 1984), 195. Allen argues that James's novels "attempt to reconcile the contradiction of woman's existence, both as sign and as conscious subject" (1). She therefore reads Maggie's struggle as semiotic and representational, rather than psychological and visual.

5. As Paul B. Armstrong, *The Phenomenology of Henry James* (Chapel Hill: University of North Carolina Press, 1983), and John Bayley, "Love and Knowledge: *The Golden Bowl*," in *The Characters of Love* (New York: Basic Books, 1960), 205–62, have subtly argued, *The Golden Bowl* enacts a drama of knowledge between self and other. Both critics focus on how unknowability structures that drama: Arm-

strong demonstrating the "opacity" of the other, and even of the self, to the self in *The Golden Bowl*, and Bayley arguing that Maggie's power rests in her refusal either to know or to be known. My focus will on be on dangers of, not the barriers to, knowing. Rather than describing the self's separateness from others, I will demonstrate its deep and necessary dependence upon them.

6. Carolyn Porter, *Seeing and Being: The Plight of the Participant Observer in Emerson, James, Adams, and Faulkner* (Middletown, Conn.: Wesleyan University Press, 1981), argues that through Maggie's recognition of her roles as seer and seen James exposes a commodified society and a reified world: "For what people see, and the way they are seen, taken together, constitute social reality in this novel" (155).

7. For discussions of the gaze, see note 49 to the introduction of this book. Although the Lacanian, psychoanalytic framework that informs these discussions differs markedly from the functionalist paradigm I am describing, both accounts of seeing connect perception, power, and identity.

8. Of course, as Strether's example shows, none of Maggie's perceptions are purely "external"; rather, they are visual texts that result from the interaction of environment and eye. I use the term here and below to distinguish between what William James calls "*the consciousness of particular material things present to sense*" (2:722) and those "mental" or "internal" images not directly prompted by sensational responses to objects or events outside the body.

9. Gabriel Pearson, "The novel to end all novels: *The Golden Bowl*," in *The Air of Reality: New Essays on Henry James*, ed. John Goode (London: Metheun, 1972), 307. In contrast, see Bayley for a vivid description of the novel's physicality, 218–19.

10. Although he is not discussing the visual, Michael S. Kearns's description of Isabel Archer's "subjective world," in *Metaphors of Mind in Fiction and Psychology* (Lexington: University of Kentucky Press, 1987), captures this materiality: "The internal realm is as active and functional as the external. In the Jamesian world, perception is never disembodied but is always a sensual experience, the most important component of the individual's sentient life" (190). Kearns uses "functional" in its common, rather then its historical, sense.

11. Ruth Bernard Yeazell, *Language and Knowledge in the Late Novels of Henry James* (Chicago: University of Chicago Press, 1976), 12.

12. John Carlos Rowe, *The Theoretical Dimensions of Henry James* (Madison: University of Wisconsin Press, 1984), 194.

13. James addresses these representational issues as such in both "Winchelsea, Rye, and 'Denis Duval' " and "Within the Rim." See Chapter 4. For discussions of late nineteenth-century art's interest in the visible materiality of writing, see Michael Fried, *Realism, Writing, Disfiguration: On Thomas Eakins and Stephen Crane* (Chicago: University of Chicago Press, 1987), and Walter Benn Michaels, *The Gold Standard and the Logic of Naturalism: American Literature at the Turn of the Century* (Berkeley: University of California Press, 1987).

14. This scene is presented retrospectively; in fact, Maggie seems to recall it visually: "It fell for retrospect into a succession of moments that were *watchable* still" (24:11). As I will demonstrate below, such mental images are often the visual means by which Maggie moves toward self-consciousness. However, in this case, James's tenses make it clear that Maggie's visual analysis of these "moments" occurs primarily on the Matcham day itself rather than when she recalls it.

15. Mark Seltzer, *Henry James and the Art of Power* (Ithaca: Cornell University Press, 1984), points out the importance of, but not the ambivalence about, self-awareness in the novel when he argues that "the characters are perpetually 'watching each other' (2:239), but Maggie, above all, 'watched herself' (2:141) and gets the others to watch themselves, to adjust and to conform 'autonomously' to the normative vision of the marriages that her power of mild insistence imposes" (65).

16. See Nicola Bradbury's comment in *Henry James: The Later Novels* (Oxford: Clarendon Press, 1979) that the "lumber-room image is domestic, not portentous" (164). However, she argues that the room is an image for the "impenetrability . . . [of] other persons," rather than of the self (164).

17. Cf. Freud's description of the way the contents of the unconscious draw similar material to them: "Moreover, it is a mistake to emphasize only the repulsion which operates from the direction of the conscious upon what is to be repressed; quite as important is the attraction exercised by what was primally repressed upon everything with which it can establish a connection," "Repression" in *The Standard Edition of the Complete Psychological Works of Sigmund Freud*, ed. and trans. James Strachey, 24 vols. (London: Hogarth Press and The Institute of Psychoanalysis, 1953–74), 14:148. What is *not* Freudian about Henry James's description is the consciousness (even self-consciousness) of the repression and the easy access to the "repressed" that is granted (Maggie's opening and reopening the door).

18. William James discusses both extreme examples of this avoidance phenomenon (cases of hysteria) and "normal" instances, including a transparent description of himself, which, although it is not confined to strictly visual attention, closely resembles Maggie's methods of distraction: "I know a person, for example, who will poke the fire, set chairs straight, pick dust-specks from the floor, arrange his table, snatch up the newspaper, take down any book which catches his eye, trim his nails, waste the morning *anyhow*, in short, and all without premeditation,—simply because the only thing he *ought* to attend to is the preparation of a noon-day lesson in formal logic which he detests. Anything but *that*!" (1:398). On the history of psychological theories of the unconscious, see Henri F. Ellenberger, *The Discovery of the Unconscious: The History and Evolution of Dynamic Psychiatry* (New York: Basic Books, 1970).

19. In opposition, see Phillip Sicker, *Love and the Quest for Identity in the Fiction of Henry James* (Princeton: Princeton University Press, 1980), who argues that others threaten the Jamesian self with dissolution, not with fixity.

20. On the resurrection of buried metaphor in James, see Yeazell, *Language and Knowledge*, 30–32. Yeazell's astute analysis does not, however, always hold true. She notes that "the buried meanings which surface in James's late novels seem to arise out of an unconscious more cultural than personal—a shared unconscious of verbal origins and connections, not of private and arbitrary associations" (30–31). James also uses mental, not metaphoric, images to portray the workings of a particular mind, a mind that is, however, culturally constituted.

21. Maggie gives up consistency very early in her half of the novel: "Maggie's actual reluctance to ask herself with proportionate sharpness why she had ceased to take comfort in the sight of it represented accordingly a lapse from that ideal consistency on which her moral comfort almost at any time depended" (24:6). For a fascinating discussion of the nineteenth century's anxious interest in a consistency between past and present, see Alexander Welsh, *George Eliot and Blackmail* (Cambridge: Harvard University Press, 1985).

22. Allen, *A Woman's Place*: "I am suggesting that the importance of central female consciousnesses in James's novels lies in the development of the conflict of the woman as sign and as self" (7).

23. On the blush as a sign of knowledge, see Christopher Ricks, *Keats and Embarrassment* (Oxford: Clarendon Press, 1974), and Ruth

Bernard Yeazell, "Podsnappery, Sexuality, and the English Novel," *Critical Inquiry* 9 (1982): 339–57.

24. Mark Seltzer's " 'The Vigilance of "Care" ': Love and Power in *The Golden Bowl*," in *Henry James and the Art of Power*, 59–95, describes "a criminal continuity" (66) between love and power and argues that its "vigilance of 'care' " is, in fact, a policing supervision. Other recent analyses of the power structures in *The Golden Bowl* focus primarily on the Ververs as capitalists, arguing that the novel represents a reified world. See, for example, Jean-Christophe Agnew, "The Consuming Vision of Henry James," in *Critical Essays in American History, 1880–1980*, ed. Richard Wightman Fox and T. J. Jackson Lears (New York: Pantheon Books, 1983), 65–100, and Porter, "Henry James: Visionary Being," in *Seeing and Being*, 121–64.

25. For some other discussions of silence in later James in general and *The Golden Bowl* in particular, see Nicola Bradbury, "The Unspeakable and the Unsayable," in *Henry James*, 13–35; Carren Kaston, *Imagination and Desire in the Novels of Henry James* (New Brunswick: Rutgers University Press, 1984), 138–41; H. Peter Stowell, *Literary Impressionism: James and Chekhov* (Athens: University of Georgia Press, 1980), 230–34; Phillip Weinstein, *Henry James and the Requirements of the Imagination* (Cambridge: Harvard University Press, 1971), 171–73. On waiting, see Yeazell, "The Syntax of Knowing," 16–36, in *Language and Knowledge*.

26. See Seltzer, *The Art of Power*: "Maggie's empathetic improvisations—her ability to put herself at once in the place of victim and in the place of victimizer—are the measure of her power" (71).

27. See, for example, her appearance, dressed in the clothing of the past, at Amerigo's fireside in Book 1. Charlotte's ability to present herself visually rivals Marie de Vionnet's.

28. Sallie Sears, *The Negative Imagination: Form and Perspective in the Novels of Henry James* (Ithaca: Cornell University Press, 1968), captures this duality when she calls Maggie "the tiger in the lamb" (192). However, Sears sees Maggie's split as, at least in part, one between a private and a public self (204). As I have argued throughout, public and private selves are not separately constituted in James.

29. Immediately after this Maggie follows Charlotte's gaze as it turns toward the other author of her fate: Adam.

30. On the logic of Charlotte's suffering, see Daniel Mark Fogel, *Henry James and the Structure of the Romantic Imagination* (Baton Rouge: Louisiana State University Press, 1981), 117; Donald L. Mull, *Henry*

James's 'Sublime Economy': Money as Symbolic Center in the Fiction (Middletown, Conn.: Wesleyan University Press, 1973), 160; Sears, *The Negative Imagination*, 178, 205.

31. See James's description of Adam at home: "He had left the table but was seated near the fire with two or three of the morning papers and the residuum of the second and third posts on a stand beside him—more even than the usual extravagance, as Maggie's glance made out, of circulars, catalogues, advertisements, announcements of sales, foreign envelopes and foreign handwritings that were as unmistakable as foreign clothes" (24:30).

32. Bayley, *The Characters of Love*, 241–42.

33. Laurence B. Holland, *The Expense of Vision: Essays on the Craft of Henry James* (1964; reprint, Baltimore: Johns Hopkins University Press, 1982), 406.

34. See Allen, *A Woman's Place*: "However triumphal, Maggie remains image [*sic*] in her relation to her world—her achieved selfhood expresses most fully her alienation from her social appearance" (179). On the intimacy of power, see Seltzer, *The Art of Power*, 70–81.

CHAPTER 3

The Fall into History

The Visual Landscape
of The American Scene

INCREASINGLY IN RECENT YEARS, literary criticism has moved away from using nonfictional and especially autobiographical writings as historical sources for literary texts and toward exploring the textual nature of all writing. The second half of *The Historical Eye* has just such an exploration as its project, investigating the ways in which James portrays himself as perceiver in a travel memoir, *The American Scene*, and two essays, "Winschelsea, Rye, and 'Denis Duval' " and "Within the Rim." The functional perception that structures James's fiction is at work in these nonfictional texts. As with Strether and Maggie, the process of perception becomes the means of survival for James's changing self. For us as literary critics, recognition of that visual process becomes a way to avoid both a formalism that divorces author and text from historical, material circumstances and a determinism that views art and artist as the contingent products of history and culture. The mutually creative, reciprocal engagement between perceiver and environment that James describes provides an alternative model for the writer's relation to his or her culture. Ensconced, in turn, in a rapidly changing, increasingly consumerist America; an East Sussex landscape where the lives of past artists can be read palimpsestically; and an English island nation whose integrity is threatened by war, James depicts neither self nor setting as a separable ground.

In *The American Scene* James represents himself as an interested perceiver who constructs sights that suit his needs. Like his characters, James struggles to survive in an environment through seeing. This visual struggle is also, and importantly, a temporal one. James shares Maggie's recognition that without some connection between past and present, identity is lost.

That identity is threatened by the changes James sees in America. Henry James's novels treat the social construction of self; *The American Scene* examines the relationship between individual and national identities. James's focus on environment switches from the social realm of personal interactions to broader questions about the self's relationships with culture—and with nature. Accordingly, he directs his perceptual attention to the American landscape.

My analysis of Jamesian visual perception in *The American Scene* is divided into three sections: "Perceiver," "Picture," and "History." The first section, "Perceiver," delineates the perceptual tradition that James inherits and modifies. Associationism had provided the primary critical justification for early American art. Such art seemed an impossibility in a country made suspicious of representation and the imagination by its Puritan heritage and in an era when the highest art was historical, and America a land without history. However, those who defended nativist American painting and literature argued that not only could such art morally educate its audience, but that association would enrich and elevate American scenes formerly barren of culture and history. Although a historical landscape is precisely what James wants to see in America, the atomistic passivity of the associationist model is, as Chapters 1 and 2 have shown, inadequate to the active, interested, streamlike nature of Jamesian visual perception. His perceptual excursions into the American scene therefore entail a functionalist reworking of associationism.

The activity of Strether's and Maggie's functional perceptions save both their identities and James's narrative from following the straightforward chronological pattern that makes for psychological determinism and literary naturalism. In *The American Scene*, James, too, remembers rather than replicates the past. Instead of automatically, passively following the path of association, he tries, attentively, selectively, to weave the past into the present. The transitional figure of Ruskin—at once a major influence on early American art and a theorist whose unorthodox active visual associationism has gone largely unrecognized—is central here. In his emphasis on visual activity, Ruskin anticipates functionalism. Nonetheless, the selfish, interested seeing described by psychologists like William James, for whom all activities are Darwinian survival tactics, is alien to the Ruskinian perceiver. Comparison between Ruskinian and Jamesian seeing helps to define both the early nineteenth-century inheritance and the twentieth-century interests of the latter.

The next section, "Picture," analyzes the landscape pictures that this interested perceiver creates, showing how James draws on Hudson River structures for his model and why he rejects more contemporary pictorial structures. Because of their capacity to represent time spatially, their place in James's visual memory, and their connection with the American writers of his boyhood, Hudson River pictures are, for James, landscapes of the past. By placing himself in the tradition of the visual and literary artists of his childhood, James seeks to see an American landscape that satisfies his adult need to connect his present with his past. Because James is claiming an American artistic history, the condescending tone of *Hawthorne* (1879) is, as Furth notes, missing from *The American Scene*.[1] Writing in 1879 for a British audience, James tried to prove his literary ability by downplaying his American identity. In 1904, no longer desperate to keep his distance, he attempts to locate himself within American cultural history by placing himself visually within the American landscape.

The final section of the chapter, "History," explores James's complexly motivated interest in these historical landscapes. James's visual search for a temporally deep American landscape is a quest for a historically integrated personal, public, and professional self. Appalled by the rapidity and ruthlessness of American "progress," James is nonetheless prompted by his interest in narrative to search visually for the human story in the landscape. Even as he seeks to preserve the past, James focuses on the marks of change. This ambivalence about the American landscape's fall into history is played out in James's uneasy perceptual attempts to balance nature and culture in his American scenes. Yet even this historical unease is part of James's heritage, as examination of the writings and paintings of the first major American landscapist, Thomas Cole, reveals. Cole's dissatisfaction with both the primitive purity of an untouched nature and the destructive progress of human civilization is echoed in James's constant search for, and disappointment in, the human side of the American landscape. In examining the relations between nature and culture over time, both artists explore the intertwining of their identities with their environments. Like Cole before him, James inscribes himself as artist in the landscape and, in doing so, confronts the problem of his own death.

By visually creating his historical American landscapes, James attempts to avoid the destruction of America's and his own identities. But the longer James remains in twentieth-century America, the less able he is to construct these visual bridges between past and present (hence my chapter's primary—though not exclusive—focus on the early chapters of *The American Scene*). In America the selfish eye of functionalism threatens to become the destructive gaze of consumerism. James's participation in the American commodification of the landscape is played out visually in *The American Scene*. James ends by viewing America from the detached, ahistorical position of the twentieth-century American railroad traveler.

Perceiver

As perceiver of the American scene, James is, like his characters, directed by self-interest. William James argues that, at base, "each of us is animated by a *direct feeling of regard for his own pure principle of individual existence*" (1:303). That individual existence is, however, far from pure: "It is simply my total empirical selfhood . . . my historic Me, a collection of objective facts" (1:306). The attempt to retain this "historic Me," this collection of past experiences, is what prompts Henry James to fashion his perceptual pictures of America. By seeing the past in America's present landscape, James can preserve his own identity over time.

The deep interest in retaining a recognizable self that shapes James's American scenes is figured in his physical relation with the landscape. The intimacy he anticipates—"I think with a great appetite, in advance, of the chance once more, to *lie on the ground*, on an American hillside, on the edge of American woods, in the manner of my youth"[2]—is partially achieved at Chocorua when he appears on native ground as Rip Van Winkle, a character James associates with childhood and with the " 'Hudson River School' of landscape art."

> I woke up, by a quick transition, in the New Hampshire mountains, in the deep valleys and the wide woodlands, on the forest-fringed slopes, the far-seeing crests of the

high places, and by the side of the liberal streams and
the lonely lakes; things full, at first, of the sweetness of
belated recognition, that of the sense of some bedimmed
summer of the distant prime flushing back into life and
asking to give again as much as possible of what it had
given before—all in spite, too, of much unacquaintedness,
of the newness, to my eyes, through the mild September
glow, of the particular rich region. (13)

Like Rip, James awakens after an absence of twenty years
deeply ensconced in (note the insistent "in . . . in . . . on . . .
by") a landscape that is at once new and old.[3] In Irving's tale,
Rip returns to his hometown, which is the same yet different,
to find that he is newly old (having slept for twenty years)
and forever young (he mistakes his son, also named Rip, for
himself).

James's appearance as Rip Van Winkle and his turning to
Hudson River models might be read as expressions of longing
for the happy, careless days of America's, and the American
James's, infancy. Rip, by sleeping through America's coming
of age in the Revolutionary War, manages to go from first to
second childhoods without ever experiencing the hardships of
adulthood.[4] Similarly, James has been accused of avoiding the
problems of American civilization in *The American Scene* by
looking to and longing for a mythical, pastoral innocence.[5]

However, Rip is "really at the bottom of it all," not because
he supplies a model for nostalgia, but because of his ambiguous
position as what James calls himself: "the restored absentee,"
a figure at once inside and outside American culture. On the
very first page of *The American Scene* he describes a setting both
known and unknown: "One's extremest youth had been full
of New York, and one was absurdly finding it again, meeting
it at every turn, in sights, sounds, smells, even in the chaos of
confusion and change" (1). The "it" that James finds again is
not just the New York that he keeps returning to in *The
American Scene*; "it" is also his youth. As John Quidor's eerie

illustration *The Return of Rip Van Winkle* (fig. 1) makes clear, Rip's trauma is more than the shock of a changed environment. What Quidor portrays is an identity crisis: Rip's troubled gaze is directed not at the town or townspeople, but at the young Rip, his son/self. " 'God knows . . . I'm not myself—I'm somebody else,' " cries Rip in Irving's story. Alan Trachtenberg points out that "the lost and baffled Rip has a major place in our culture. . . . What is threatened is not merely this or that memory or monument, but the integrity of time and the wholeness of self."[6] In creating his American landscapes, James struggles to preserve a continuous self.

The interdependency of identity and environment which we can trace in *The American Scene* resembles what John Barrell calls the "sense of place" in John Clare's poetry.[7] Barrell argues that Clare began with a "circular" sense of landscape: the terrain of his parish radiated out from his village as an open, uniform space. He knew this centered world intimately, almost exclusively. Filled with familiar, local detail, the land provided the materials of both Clare's poetry and the poet's own identity. However, the influence of picturesque ideas of landscape on poetry, along with the Enclosure Acts, worked to fragment Clare's sense of place. Individual landscapes came to be seen in terms of general, abstract patterns. Barrell describes the picturesque perceiver, who, standing at a high vantage point, looks rapidly *over* the scene to the horizon before circling back to the foreground, as visually imposing a standard pattern that obscures the particular features of any landscape. Similarly, enclosure transformed the individual parish into one in a series of identical points on a map, stops on a road, or, eventually, a railway line. Both of these modes of perceiving helped to break down Clare's sense of the warmly known landscape of his past, a landscape that, in turn, "knew" him. And, Barrell suggests, they helped to break down Clare as well.

Like Clare, James wants a personally centered, readable landscape. Both writers' identities are bound up with the problem

Fig. 1. John Quidor, The Return of Rip Van Winkle, c. 1849. Courtesy of National Gallery of Art, Washington; Andrew W. Mellon Collection

of placing themselves in a home, a countryside with a familiar past. A landscape created after a general pattern that suppresses local detail is necessarily insufficient to this task of self-identification. Hence James's frequent Clare-like dislocation and detachment in *The American Scene*. For example, his railroad travels, during which he views the landscape from a detached position and participates in the equalization of the American countryside into a uniform series of points, often leave him disconcerted and alienated. However, unlike Clare, James can be at home in a landscape without being located literally at its center. Sometimes he does look out from the middle of a scene; in other instances we follow him as he walks deep into the landscape; elsewhere he simply views the "embowered" center from a lofty vantage point. A scene in which he might potentially insert himself will suffice. Further, Barrell's description of picturesque seeing as a delocalizing process does not hold true for *The American Scene* because James, like the Hudson River painters who first pictured these landscapes, does not sacrifice detail to overall recession. When he describes a landscape from a high vantage point, the eye may indeed be drawn to the horizon, but the emphasis is on the circling perception of detail.

This emphasis on local detail[8] and excursive sight has its source in Ruskin, whose writings deeply influenced American artists and art critics. Roger Stein speculates that "probably the only English authors whose works were more popular with American readers and publishers were novelists like Scott and Dickens."[9] Certainly, as Stein shows, the *Crayon*, the house journal for the Hudson River school, was virtually a Ruskinian publication.[10] James's connections to this American associationist tradition of landscape painting and writing are discernible in his perceptual resemblances to Ruskin.

That James knew Ruskin's writings well is not news.[11] But if Ruskin has been recognized as "the greatest single source of James's aesthetic," the nature of this influence has been misunderstood because of the tendency to label Ruskin's theory of art "notoriously tortuous and contradictory."[12] Fortunately, Elizabeth Helsinger has clarified the nature of Ruskin's perceptual psychology by taking seriously the possibility of an associationist aesthetic for painting.[13] Although the relevance of associationism to early nineteenth-century literary aesthetics has long been accepted, nineteenth-century art critics who, like Ruskin and James, judged a painting on the basis of its ability to arouse "associations" have been criticized for ignoring the work's technical and structural properties in favor of its literary content. Helsinger shows that what has not been understood is that Ruskin employs an unorthodox *visual* associationism, which, I will argue, in its emphasis on activity, moves beyond the passivity of associationism, foreshadowing functionalism.

Helsinger describes how romantic critics, using an early associationist model, distinguished between reading a poem and seeing a painting: "Literature, they argued, directly presents a certain train of associations. Its order is essentially the order of an imaginative mind, first the poet's, then the reader's. Looking at a painting merely stimulates such a train of associated ideas" (183). This is the understanding of associationism that informs early nineteenth-century American art and aesthetics: the sight of a painting sparks a series of literary associations that moves the mind of the passive spectator away from the visual experience. Similarly, Bryant's poetry presents composed landscapes, arranged so as to prompt associations. In contrast, Ruskin argues that seeing a painting entails an active, extended visual engagement. It is not a question of seeing and *then* associating; the eye's movement over a painting and the mind's movement through a series of associations are one single and dynamic activity.

Keeping the viewer's eye—and mind—directed on the painting results in projected entrance into the picture-space.[14] This entry into the landscape is exactly what James attempts to achieve with his pictures of America. His American pictures are filled with lights that "glimmer," shapes that "loom" in the "gloaming," with "iridescence," with the autumn glow that gives a mysterious depth to objects—with, in short, movement. And what moves are simultaneously the scenes, in their intricate depth of historical and personal association, and the eye and mind of the observer. By traveling visually into the landscape, James can analyze these scenes perceptually.

Let us compare a Ruskinian and a Jamesian landscape. In *Modern Painters I*, Ruskin describes how nature presents a landscape to the eye:

> Every one of those broad spaces she would linger over in protracted delight, teaching you fresh lessons in every hair's breadth of it, and pouring her fulness of invention into it, until the mind lost herself in following her: now fringing the dark edge of the shadow with a tufted line of level forest; now losing it for an instant in a breath of mist; then breaking it with the white gleaming angle of a narrow brook; then dwelling upon it again in a gentle, mounded, melting undulation, over the other side of which she would carry you down into a dusty space of soft crowded light, with the hedges and the paths and the sprinkled cottages and scattered trees mixed up and mingled together in one beautiful, delicate, impenetrable mystery, sparkling and melting, and passing away into the sky, without one line of distinctness, or one instant of vacancy. (3:332–33)

Here is James describing the Saco River Valley:

> I went down into the valley—that was an impression to woo by stages; I walked beside one of those great fields of standing Indian corn which make, to the eye, so perfect a note for the rest of the American rural picture, throwing the conditions back as far as our past permits, rather than forward, as so many other things do, into the age to come.

The maker of these reflections betook himself at last, in any case, to an expanse of rock by a large bend of the Saco, and lingered there under the infinite charm of the place. The rich, full lapse of the river, the perfect brownness, clear and deep, as of liquid agate, in its wide swirl, the large indifferent ease in its pace and motion, as of some great benevolent institution smoothly working; all this, with the sense of the deepening autumn about, gave I scarce know what pastoral nobleness to the scene, something raising it out of the reach of even the most restless of analysts. The analyst in fact could scarce be restless here; the impression, so strong and so final, persuaded him perfectly to peace. This, on September Sunday mornings, was what American beauty *should* be; it filled to the brim its idea and its measure. . . . It was the great, gay river, singing as it went, like some reckless adventurer, good-humoured for the hour and with his hands in his pockets, that argued the whole case and carried everything assentingly before it. (28–29)

Like Ruskin, James describes an active, engaged perceiver. James does not close his eyes and allow his associations to take him away from the present landscape. Rather, by focusing on the Indian corn, which he associates with America's "ancient" peoples, he is able to enact the visual associationism that Ruskin argues for: eye and mind move together. Spatial and temporal depth intersect in James's picture of a "deepening autumn" valley. The history-filled Saco Valley permits his eye to travel calmly, an action figured here by the river's motion, which, for all its recklessness, does not partake of the frantic American hurry that James abhors. Instead, its "rich, full lapse" and "wide swirl," the "large indifferent ease in its pace and motion," resemble the motion-filled stillness that James describes elsewhere as "iridescence." Even the brownness of the river is not flat and opaque, but "clear and deep as of liquid agate." This calm swirl follows the pace at which nature leads the eye over the "gentle, mounded, melting undulations" of Ruskin's landscape.

James's relaxation in the Saco Valley does not, however, mean that he becomes a passive perceiver. The analyst remains analytic. He is carried "assentingly," not passively, into the landscape. Further, while the activity of such seeing is Ruskinian, its selfish, interested nature is not. In the Ruskin passage, nature guides the eye and mind into and about the scene. The structure of the natural landscape instructs by directing perceptual activity ("teaching you fresh lessons . . . she would carry you down"). The spectator's preconceptions, needs, and desires must be put aside in order to see and learn: "The mind lost itself in following her." Nature will always remain superior: an "impenetrable mystery," teaching what is necessary, but never becoming fully knowable.

In contrast, James's need to perceive the past in the present directs and informs his visual picture of a deep historical space. The James passage begins by emphasizing the perceiver ("I") who initiates the motion (he walks into the valley and along the rows of Indian corn) and selects his scene. Perception must be achieved by his interested activity: "an impression to woo by stages." More powerful than Ruskin's spectator, the perceiver of the Saco Valley resembles William James's perceptual artist, who with attention sculpts a world: "Millions of items of the outward order are present to my senses which never properly enter into my experience. Why? Because they have no *interest* for me. . . . Only those items which I *notice* shape my mind. . . . Interest . . . *makes* experience more than it is made by it" (1:380–81). Making his own experience in the Saco Valley is the "maker of these reflections," Henry James, who visually creates his American environment. Accordingly, James's nature is less powerful than Ruskin's. Not only is the river humanized (shades of the pathetic fallacy!), it must argue its case and gain the spectator's assent, illustrating William James's assertion that "*my experience is what I agree to attend to*" (1:380). In the Saco Valley, the very activity of Henry James's

visual attention puts him at ease, able to picture a deeply historical America in which he can locate himself as an American.

Picture

While Ruskin's and William James's perceptual theories illuminate the activity and intimacy of James's visual engagement with the landscape, the painters and writers of James's
childhood, themselves influenced by Ruskin, supply the structural model for his American scenes. In 1904, James returns
to his American artistic predecessors, reworking the earlier
pictorial tradition visually.

Hudson River painting provides a link between James's past
and his present, allowing him to approach an America that he
barely recognizes. But this perceptual connection is difficult—
indeed, often impossible—for James to achieve. Even the historical landscape of the Saco Valley is a perceptual picture he
must "woo by stages." Like Maggie, James must struggle to
create the visual pictures that will ensure his survival over time.

What frustrates James's search for a historical landscape, and
thus an enduring identity, is the fact that most American scenes
do not permit the past's presence. Because America brutally
erases its past, its landscapes are ahistorical.[15] As Ruskin had
pointed out in "The Lamp of Memory" chapter of *The Seven
Lamps of Architecture*, disregard for the visible endurance of the
past entails a disrespect for the lives of individuals. Architectural, national, and personal identities come together in Ruskin's description of the "good man's" grief at the destruction
of his home, a description that uncannily foretells James's own
reaction to the destruction of the houses of his childhood
(8:225–27).[16] A "high, square, impersonal structure" stands in
the place of the "rudely, the ruthlessly suppressed birth-house"
in Washington Square (91).[17] When James returns to his old
home on Ashburton Place in Boston, a week after having vis-
ited the house, he finds only "a gaping void, the brutal ef-

facement, at a stroke, of every related object, of the whole precious past" (229). The house has been destroyed in order to make space for a new building. The shallowness of the American scene means that the present *replaces* the past. There is no depth where the two can coexist and enrich one another. Instead, there is constant, frantic change.

James complains throughout *The American Scene* about the glare of the harsh American sun, which equalizes and flattens, giving "the eternal impression of things all in a row and of a single thickness" (294).[18] The blinding glare makes the distinctive, the specific, the local indistinguishable: "American life having been organized, *ab ovo*, with an hostility to the town-nook which has left no scrap of provision for eyes needing on occasion a refuge from the general glare" (294). James's choice of the word "refuge" here is significant; such impenetrable landscapes provide no place for the spectator. In contrast, at Philadelphia, perception allows him to become a part of the American scene: "I can but continue to lose myself, for these connections, in my *whole* sense of the intermission, as I have called it, of the glare. The mellower light prevailed, somehow, *all* that fine Philadelphia morning" (295).

This mellow light characterizes James's Hudson River pictures. That what James sees in America should take this form may seem somewhat surprising, given the general consensus that he disdained American painting. Indeed, his remarks about the Hudson River School in *The American Scene* seem at first to confirm such a judgment. Describing a scene in the Chocorua Mountains, he speaks of a situation interfused with "every typical triumph of the American landscape 'school,' now as rococo as so many squares of ingenious wool-work, but the remembered delight of our childhood" (18). Hudson River painting is, it seems, like "wool-work," a craft, not an art. American pictures delight only children.

However, a closer examination of the embroidery metaphor indicates that James does not use it simply to condescend to the primitive state of American art. He employs images of needlework to describe the way a collection of "impression-istic" pictures creates one of the "two or three of these strong patches of surface-embroidery" that give depth to the "thin-ness" of American life (45); the "iridescence," "bestitching" the Quaker drab of Philadelphia (284–85); how the university's presence animates Baltimore: "the embroidery of the fine can-vas turned thick and rich" (317); the way the canvas of Charles-ton awaits spring's embroidery; and how, faced with the loss of well-known Boston buildings, one finds one's self "free to picture them, to embroider them, at one's ease—to tangle them up in retrospect and make the real romantic claim for them" (228). Needlework adds color, variety, and depth to otherwise flat American scenes. James turns repeatedly to metaphors of embroidery because it is the humble craft of making three-dimensional pictures.

James's attempts to regard the American landscape as a tex-tured surface also point to the textual nature of Jamesian per-ception.[19] As he says explicitly, James reads "into" as well as "out" of America (291). His perceptions of America are neither images imprinted upon his retina from without nor indepen-dent creations of some inner eye. James's landscape pictures are worked sites.

While these visual landscapes do not illustrate some original, innocent relationship between seer and scene, they *are* chil-dren's pictures in that, by turning to a style of painting that flourished more than a half-century before his 1904 trip, James returns not only to America's youth, but also to his own. Hud-son River School paintings are part of the personal framework through which James naturally apprehends America. His early perceptions of these pictures helped structure his visual habits. In composing his own American landscapes, James does not always follow exactly what has come to be known as the Hud-son River formula; that is, he does not invariably look down from a lofty vantage point past near-looking detail and framing trees toward water in the middle distance and mountains ascending into mist at the horizon (fig. 2)—although sometimes he does. However, James's landscapes are Hudson River in their emphasis on the *depth* of the picture space. James's Ruskinian interest in the spectator's entry into the landscape is shared with his American predecessors.[20] Asher Durand, the major painter-theorist of the Hudson River School, maintains: "That is a fine picture which at once takes possession of you—draws you into it—you traverse it—breathe its atmosphere—feel its sunshine, and you repose in its shade" (fig. 3).[21] In using atmosphere and light to deepen his scenes, James also visually echoes Anglo-American painting's fascination with weather, air, sun, and sky. His practice is aptly described by Durand, who contends that atmosphere is "the power which defines and measures space. . . . It is that which above all other agencies, carries us into the picture, instead of allowing us to be detained in front of it."[22] As Barbara Novak notes in *American Painting of the Nineteenth Century*, the Hudson River painters relied on a linear sense of form, yet also "made use of the perceptual and atmospheric potentials of the painterly."[23] Similarly, in employing an atmospheric, painterly "glow" along with vividly highlighted details, James combines "a painterly vision with a linear feeling for form."[24]

James also follows Hudson River painters in the ends to which he uses pictorial depth. The notion that one might elevate the aesthetic and moral importance of a landscape by making it historical was an idea that American painters imported from Europe. Their model was the classic Claudian landscape, which conveys temporal depth both by its representation of Greek and Roman scenes and by its spatializing of time through a recession into three planes, harmonized by a mellow golden tone. However, as Karl Kroeber points out, Claude "detemporalized story and history. . . . His paintings

Fig. 2. *Asher Brown Durand*, View of the Hudson River Valley, *1851. Courtesy of Herbert F. Johnson Museum of Art, Cornell University; Ernest I. White Endowment Fund*

Fig. 3. Asher Brown Durand, *Genesee Oaks*, 1860. Courtesy of Memorial Art Gallery of the University of Rochester; gift of the Women's Council in honor of Harris K. Prior

. . . coalesce sequentiality into the unity of a scenic stillness."[25] History is fixed in amber. Although Hudson River painters employed Claudian techniques to show that America's history was worthy of art, the differences between European and American landscapes meant that certain adaptations were necessary. The traditional deep structure and golden tone were adopted intact, but the "scenic stillness" of the classical landscape was disrupted in American scenes. Hudson River painters exchanged the generalized Claudian mythological landscape for local, detailed American scenes.[26] Ancient trees and "primitive" Indians took the place of ruined castles and abbeys; autumnal variations in the American foliage marked the passage of the seasons; mountains embodied geologic ages; painting cycles conveyed epochal change. As these examples indicate, such details gave an immediacy to the temporal change portrayed. In fact, time was often displayed in the American landscape as the future, rather than the past. What Novak calls "Man's Traces: Axe, Train, Figure" both mark these American landscapes with the actions of the present and imply the new forms that will follow.

The fact that America often seemed to be rushing toward the new at an alarming pace meant that pictorial structures were used not only to portray historical change but also in an attempt to control and order it, as in Durand's *Progress* (1853), where smoke from a train, steamboats, and factories blend peacefully into the natural clouds.[27] However, the very proximity of such change made its control difficult—in America, axes were agents of destruction, not antiques.

The importance of these methods to a writer who, as Winner says, "at times, . . . almost equated history and art,"[28] can be seen in a Jamesian picture that is Hudson River both in technique and setting: the description of "An Old Country House," near Sunnyside, Washington Irving's home. Having complained that America is organized so as to blind itself to the "golden truth . . . that production takes time, and that the production of interest, in particular, takes *most* time" (153), James finds relief in the "charming old historic house of the golden Sunday," with the "wide north porch," like a "high, deep gallery" which makes it a "refuge" in America's "raw medium" (153). The porch, by adding an additional layer or plane to the picture, provides the penetralia that James so misses in American buildings. The house's depth is at once spatial and temporal:

> I know not what dignity of old afternoons suffused with what languor seems to me always, under the murmur of American trees and by the lap of American streams, to abide in these mild shades; there are combinations with depths of congruity beyond the plummet, it would seem, even of the most restless of analysts, and rather than try to say why my whole impression here melted into general iridescence of a past of Indian summers hanging about mild ghosts half asleep, in hammocks, over still milder novels, I would renounce altogether the art of refining. For the iridescence consists, in this connection, of a shimmer of association that still more refuses to be reduced to terms; some sense of legend, of aboriginal mystery, with a still earlier past for its dim background and the insistent idea of the River as above all romantic for its warrant. (153–54)

The American obsession with gold as money is replaced by a deep golden glow. Ichabod Crane, the insatiable consumer who sees landscape only as a commodity, is banished from Sleepy Hollow. This glowing gold exists in the medium of time, not time as James sees it elsewhere in America—a frenzied present sweeping away all signs of the past—but rather, as a spatialized deep present that *contains* the past. The scene, in Jamesian argot, "goes back." Hence its "iridescence," a word that, like "golden," James uses, as he does in the Saco Valley description, to depict scenes in which he finds a conjunction of past and present that he can admire. "Iridescence" is a three-dimensional surface, a stillness filled with spatial and temporal motion. In referring to iridescence's "shimmer of association," Henry James is following his brother and other psychologists who use the term to describe the spreading, changing excitations of the brain that constitute the associative stream of thought.[29] Henry James's atmospheric landscapes, like Strether's Parisian pictures, convey the full, fluid stream of perception. Iridescent with association, they recede in time and allow James to avoid both the brutal erasures of American progress and the stagnation of nostalgia. He inserts this shimmering quality in his pictures by focusing on light filtered through atmosphere. James rejects the broad, harsh American noonday sun for, near Sunnyside, an afternoon glow, or, elsewhere, a "gloaming" in which he detects "glimmers."

Before we can understand fully how and why these pictures work for James, we need to look at other painterly models that he tries—and rejects—in *The American Scene*. James might have been expected, in 1904, to turn to contemporary painting rather than to old-fashioned Hudson River scenes. After all, *The American Scene* contains a passage frequently cited to demonstrate James's conversion to impressionism.[30] In fact, James himself classifies one of his own landscape descriptions as "a delightful little triumph of 'impressionism' " (34). He does so, however, just prior to uncovering the inadequacy of such a picture. The scene is a Cape Cod one that James sees from a train window:

> The simplification, for that immediate vision, was to a broad band of deep and clear blue sea, a blue of the deepest and clearest conceivable, limited in one quarter by its far and sharp horizon of sky, and in the other by its near and sharp horizon of yellow sand overfringed with a low woody shore; the whole seen through the contorted cross-pieces of stunted, wind-twisted, far-spreading, quite

fantastic old pines and cedars, whose bunched bristles, at the ends of long limbs, produced, against the light, the most vivid of all reminders. Cape Cod, on this showing, was exactly a pendent, pictured Japanese screen or banner; a delightful little triumph of "impressionism." (34)

James finds this impressionist picture, composed of flat bands of bright color, "delightful," but it does not serve his purposes precisely because it is so flat (even the arboreal crosspieces through which the seascape is seen become flattened out into a Japanese screen).[31] James glances at a "Boston bungalow, its verandahs still haunted with old summer-times, and so wide that the present could elbow yet not jostle the past" (34–35), but finds that this single summer habitation is not enough to humanize the scene. The landscapes's two-dimensional "simplification" has entailed an *elimination*:

> It [the Cape Cod promontory] interfered no whit, for all its purity of style, with the human, the social question always dogging the steps of the ancient contemplative person and making him, before each scene, wish really to get *into* the picture, to cross, as it were, the threshold of the frame. It never lifts, verily, this obsession of the story-seeker, however often it may flutter its wings, it may bruise its breast, against surfaces either too hard or too blank. (35)

By not interfering with the "social question," the impressionist canvas frustrates James. The painting's "purity of style" defeats his desire to figure time spatially; its flat surface hides human history and thus prevents the spectator's engagement and understanding.[32] "'The *manners*, the manners: where and what are they, and what have they to tell?'" cries James, "the story-seeker," knocking up against the two-dimensional picture plane (35). There is no way for James to enter, let alone inhabit, this unreadable American landscape. He cannot be an American here.

James finally does leave the train and enter the picture, only to find that he cannot make manners tell sufficiently. The "facts" that he finds upon entering the picture remain "hard" and "blank": "the little white houses, the feathery elms, the band of ocean blue, the stripe of sandy yellow, the tufted pines in angular silhouette, the cranberry-swamps stringed across, for the picking, like the ruled pages of ledgers" (37). However, James's inclusion of the stringed cranberry-swamps in the picture hints that he is beginning to read the signs of human activity into this ledger of New England, a hint that is confirmed when he realizes "the full pictorial and other value" of the young American boy who is his guide. Although the people James meets are silent or near-silent, their presence is sufficient for him to re-see the landscape as a soft, blonde giant: "I remember not less a longish walk, and a longer drive, into low extensions of woody, piney, pondy landscape, veined with blue inlets and trimmed, on opportunity, with blond beaches" (38). The few inhabitants of Cape Cod (and their meager activities) save the scene from impenetrability, but the landscape's history is nonetheless one of absence: "so many people had 'left' that the remaining characters, on the sketchy page, were too few to form a word" (38). The pun on "characters" pointedly textualizes the landscape; for James, the American scene and *The American Scene* are both records of human activity.

James's final picture of Cape Cod is, then, a compromise. He can make this scene tell a human story only by making the landscape itself human. It is a second-best solution that, faced with an absent human history, James turns to more than once in *The American Scene*. He has managed to exchange the hard impressionist canvas for a picture of "softness and sweetness," but the human record remains largely unwritten (38).

The dangerous potential for nostalgia in a sweet, anthropomorphized landscape, innocent of human history, makes it important to distinguish the softened Hudson River atmosphere of this scene not only from the flat impenetrability of impressionism, but also from a vague mistiness. We can do so by looking at a third sort of picture that appears in *The American Scene*: what James calls a "Hazy Hudson" landscape.

James actually describes two haze-filled views of the river in the same paragraph: one is seen from a railroad car window; the second during a visit to West Point a fortnight later. These similar landscape pictures are, significantly, prefaced by a discussion of American trains.[33] James complains bitterly about the fact that the railroad ruins the Hudson River view and destroys the American pastoral: the beautiful landscape, the rights of natural man ("the noble savage"), and the spectator's natural right of contemplation have all been violated (148–49). However, he concludes, "one must of course choose between dispensing with the ugly presence and enjoying the scenery by the aid of the same" (148). James, the railroad traveler, is complicitous with the force that destroys the landscape in order to see it (he could have taken one of the boats that, as he points out, give the same view without intruding upon the landscape). He continues to complain, however, declaring that the United States has greatly reduced the "rights of contemplation," reduced them as radically and "by quite the same argument, as those of the noble savage whom we have banished to his narrowing reservation. Letting that pass, at all events, I still remember that I was able to put, from the car-window, as many questions to the scene as it could have answered in the time even had its face been clearer to read" (148–49).

Although both the pronoun *we* and the way James's rapid movement over the landscape allows him to brush by the problem ("letting that pass") clearly betray his complicity, his railroad traveler's picture of the Hudson is far from clear.

> Its face was veiled, for the most part, in a mist of premature spring heat, an atmosphere draping it indeed

in luminous mystery, hanging it about with sun-shot sil-
ver and minimizing any happy detail, any element of the
definite, from which the romantic effect might here and
there have gained an accent. There was not an accent in
the picture from the beginning of the run to Albany to
the end—for which thank goodness! one is tempted to
say on remembering how often, over the land in general,
the accents are wrong. Yet if the romantic effect as we
know it elsewhere mostly depends on them, why *should*
that glamour have so shimmered before me in their absence? (149)

James is puzzled. He knows that a romantic landscape consists
of an accumulation of accents or details, but sees this scene as
both romantic and unaccented. Recalling how often his en-
joyment of the American landscape has been spoiled by the
intrusion of an inappropriate, crude detail, James conjectures
tentatively that American accents are by their very nature un-
romantic. This would mean that the only way to construct a
pleasing American landscape would be to erase all local details.

Upon returning to West Point two weeks later, James becomes convinced that "the suppression of detail" is the key to
creating American landscape art in "the grand style" (150).
The light and atmosphere of a mountain storm have, by blurring West Point's accents, moved it into "the geography of
the ideal, in the long perspective of the poetry of association"
and made it of a "type and tone good enough for Claude or
Turner" (150). James refers twice to the "grey water-colour
brush" (150–51) he has used here, as elsewhere in *The American
Scene*, to soften the picture. This blurring wash is, like the
"luminous mystery" of the haze, described as a valuable "sil-
ver" (149, 150), but James hints that in changing West Point's
"prose" to "poetry," something may have been lost: "I shall
recall it in the future much less as the sternest, the world over,
of all the seats of Discipline, than as some great Corot-com-
position of young, vague, wandering figures in splendidly-

classic shades" (151). This "splendidly-classic" scene has been achieved by "the suppression of detail as in the positive interest of the grand style" (150). James draws upon a distinction basic to eighteenth- and nineteenth-century landscape art—that between the grand style and the picturesque, high and low art, and, most commonly, Italianate and Dutch paintings. He finds the grey-washed picture "grand" in that it disdains the local detail or "accents" of Dutch painting in favor of an idealized, "generalized elegance" (151).

This generic landscape is pleasing enough. No coarse, inappropriate American details—like the railroad—intrude into the scene. But what James sees is at the same time far from satisfying *because* it is so vaguely pleasant. The ugly American railroad has been eliminated, but in its place we see only a Europeanized blur. Softening the harsh American glare with a haze merely keeps the specific, individual identity of the landscape hidden. Just as he has suppressed his own position as railroad traveler, James visually obscures West Point's identity as "the School of the Soldier"(151), the training ground for the type who, throughout *The American Scene*, raises uneasy associations with what he calls the "supreme holocaust" of the Civil War (369).[34] In this Hazy Hudson perception, history is the dim, fixed, mythological past, not an ongoing, changing record of specific human actions.

The full significance of eliminating local accents becomes clear only in the next scene, when James creates the Hudson River picture of "An Old Country House" that we looked at earlier. Here too there is no harsh glare, but neither is there a blurry mist. Instead, James sees a golden glow. What he perceives is not an ugly industrialized scene, nor one that has lost its particular historical value by becoming genteel and Europeanized, but a specific, detailed Hudson River picture:

> I make that point [that unaccented vagueness can be classic], for what it is worth, only to remind myself of an-

other occasion on which the romantic note sounded for me with the last intensity, and yet on which the picture swarmed with accents—as, absent or present, I must again call them—that contributed alike to its interest and to its dignity. The proof was complete, on this second Sunday, with the glow of the early summer already in possession, that affirmed detail was not always affirmed infelicity— since the scene here bristled with detail (and detail of the importance that frankly *constitutes* accent) only to the enhancement of its charm. . . . Infinitely sweet was it to gather that style, in such conditions and for the success of such effects, had not really to depend on mere kind vaguenesses, on any anxious deprecation of distinctness. (152)

The words "interest" and "dignity" are important here. With them, James balances himself between the two extremes of nineteenth-century American attitudes to art.[35] He disproves the argument that only European scenes are worthy of art by showing that the elimination of the local, American character of a scene does not dignify it. A general, Europeanized landscape cannot prompt deep interest and identification on the part of the American spectator. Yet James is hardly one of those chauvinistic Americans who argued that any American landscape must, by its very nature, be both more interesting to Americans and, by reason of America's purity, superior to any European one. Again and again American scenes fail to interest him; they are not landscapes in which he can figure himself as American. James's personal example implicitly argues that only a fully detailed American scene that unites past and present holds real interest for the American spectator. An interesting, dignified landscape is both unabashedly American *and* historical. The Hudson River combination of Claudian structure plus American detail was criticized in its own time for its unclassical American subject matter, and condescended to in later generations for its imported European compositional schema. What *The American Scene* implies is that both these criticisms reflect false conceptions of American art. An art that limits itself to European subjects cannot be American. An art that eliminates history is not art. The Hudson River program works because it composes America historically. Depth acquired through atmosphere, a light that softens without blurring, a lively stillness that allows the eye to actively follow details back into the landscape, spatial textures that embody temporal strata—all allow James to exchange flat, glaring expanses for intricately worked historical landscapes.[36]

History

Although Hudson River pictures provide James with a deep temporal structure, it is in the very historicizing of his perceptual landscapes that he parts company with American nativist painters and writers. Novak's observation that the human figure is "rarely a major protagonist in American landscape" painting sums up its limits for James.[37] Unlike the Hudson River paintings of Durand and others, James's pictures often have at their center a human dwelling.[38] Natural landscapes unmarked by human change cannot fulfill his narrative needs. Nor can he rest easily in the landscapes depicted by the American literary artists of his childhood. Describing the way "encircled waters . . . make the sacred grove and the American classic temple, the temple for the worship of the evening sky, the cult of the Indian canoe, of Fenimore Cooper, of W. C. Bryant, of the immortal water-fowl," James implies that, paradoxically, in historicizing the American landscape, these writers became timeless (17–18). They sanctified not only the American landscape, but also their own art: the "cult" is of Cooper and Bryant as well as of the canoe, sky, and water-fowl. The water-fowl (bird and poem) is "immortal"; the evening sky, and the Indian canoe become, not emblems of change, but changeless subjects of myth and objects of worship. As in the Claudian landscape, history is preserved in amber.

James's is, of course, a skewed reading of Bryant, Cooper, and Irving, whose pages are haunted by time and its effects. Yet, through such a misreading James is not only able to keep the world of his childhood intact, he is also able to hint that the American scenes of his literary predecessors are, in fact, childish. While James makes his real affection for, and debt to, earlier American artists clear in *The American Scene*, he nonetheless turns from what he regards as their static, innocent, protected world to his own temporally complex perceptions of a troubled culture—adult pictures, constructed after the Fall.[39]

Unable either to find narrative satisfaction in a purely natural landscape or to discover visual evidence of an unbroken, ongoing, human history, James's allegiances shift throughout *The American Scene* from nature to culture and back again in what he describes as a "bewildering, seesaw":[40]

> One was liable, in the States, on many a scene, to react, as it were, from the people and to throw one's self passionately on the bosom of contiguous Nature. . . . Yet, all unreasonably, when any source of interest did express itself in these mere rigorous terms, in these only—terms all of elimination, just of sea and sky and river-breast and forest and beach (the "beaches" in especial were to acquire a trick of getting on one's nerves!) that produced in turn a wanton wonder about the "human side," and a due recurrence to the fact that the human side had been from the first one's affair. (436)

This ambivalence allies James less with American nativist artists and more with his country's first major landscapist, Thomas Cole. Generally regarded as a "transitional" figure rather than a full-fledged nativist, Cole was an artist whose painting, like James's writing, was often criticized for being idealized and European rather than purely natural and American.[41] His influential 1835 "Essay on American Scenery"[42] reveals Cole's ambivalence toward both his native landscape and the civilization that was changing it—an ambivalence echoed seventy years later in *The American Scene.*

Cole's essay, an argument for the importance of rural scenery in general and American rural scenery in particular, is addressed specifically to the American spectator: "It is a subject that to every American ought to be of surpassing interest . . . it is his own land" (98). This interest has a moral basis: Nature, by bringing together past, present, and future—by being, in effect, historical—moves us beyond present, earthly concerns.

Cole's contention brings him up against major questions in early American aesthetics. If the American landscape has no associations (because America has so little history), how can it teach us about God and the good? How can an art that takes as its object an uncivilized country have the civilizing influence that is its justification? Cole answers that American scenes are literally historical; the problem is that they have not been made literarily so. The American landscape must be given associations by becoming storied. Looking down into an Arcadian "secluded valley," Cole predicts that it will be the scene of great deeds and that "poets yet unborn shall sanctify the soil" (109), thus pointing out the way for Bryant, Cooper, and Irving's artistry.

But Cole is ambivalent about culture's transformation of nature. On the one hand, he sees the landscape as a present blankness, waiting for civilization to complete it (109). The primitive wilderness needs to be made into America. On the other, he deplores the rapid disappearance of the natural landscape. America's identity, its "truly American character," lies in the wilderness that is being destroyed by the ax of civilization (109). But not only does Cole *not* call for America to return to its ideal primitive state, he seems to regard the "bar-

barism" of culture as inevitable. "This is a regret rather than a complaint; such is the road society has to travel; it may lead to refinement in the end, but the traveller who sees the place of rest close at hand, dislikes the road that has so many unnecessary windings" (109). Cole, with America, hovers between nature and culture. This is the necessary road to civilization; it winds unnecessarily. The road "may" lead its traveler, society, to refinement, but the end may also be "the place of rest"—death—for both society and its fellow traveler, Cole. *Et in Arcadia Ego.* He seems at once to assert and to beg the conclusion presented in his *Course of Empire* cycle (figs. 4–8): the primitive becomes the pastoral becomes the city becomes the ruin; civilizations rise only to fall. If Cole is ambivalent, other Americans refused the conclusion outright. Responding to *The Course of Empire*, the critic for the *New York Mirror* summed up his audience's beliefs by neatly exempting America from the proven course of history: "He has accomplished his object: which was to show what has been the history of empires and of man. Will it always be so? Philosophy and religion forbid."[43] America marks a new beginning.

The American Scene follows Cole's excursion into the landscape in a number of ways. Some of these resemblances are shared by most nineteenth-century American landscape discussions. Both James and Cole mention repeatedly America's vastness, wildness, mountains, lakes, rivers, forests (especially in autumn), and sky (especially at sunset). Their itineraries are also standard: both visit the mountains of New Hampshire and the Hudson and Connecticut Rivers. And James, like Cole, repeatedly raises the possibility of a new start for America—comparing New York to a new Venice, an elaborate set stage, waiting for history (184); Charleston to "some Venice that had never mustered" (419); Florida to the Nile "before Pharoahs and Pyramids, when everything was still to come" (462); and

Fig. 4. Thomas Cole, The Course of Empire: The Savage State, n/d. Courtesy of The New-York Historical Society, New York City

Fig. 5. Thomas Cole, The Course of Empire: The Arcadian or Pastoral State, *n/d. Courtesy of The New-York Historical Society, New York City*

Fig. 6. Thomas Cole, The Course of Empire: The Consummation State, 1835–36. Courtesy of The New-York Historical Society, New York City

Fig. 7. Thomas Cole, The Course of Empire: Destruction, 1836. Courtesy of The New-York Historical Society, New York City

Fig. 8. Thomas Cole, The Course of Empire: Desolation, 1836. Courtesy of The New-York Historical Society, New York City

California to "a sort of prepared but unconscious and inexperienced Italy, the primitive *plate*, in perfect condition, but with the impression of History all yet to be made" (462).[44]

However, unlike Cole's audience, and like Cole, James also fears that America is already marked by human failure. Worse, he fears that entering the realm of history will *necessarily* mean falling into a world of death and decay. Cole's *Expulsion from the Garden of Eden* (fig. 9) is divided between a sun-filled, serene paradise and the stormy, ravaged realm of time to which Adam and Eve have been expelled.[45] Despite the door that connects these two realms, the abyss (the Fall) between them embodies James's fear: continuity is irrevocably broken.

It is in his visual attempt to bridge the abyss of time, to reenter America as Rip Van Winkle, that James most resembles Cole. Awakening at Chocorua, he recognizes the scene as "Arcadia" (13). But James wonders what Arcadia is doing in this New England landscape, empty of human civilization. He discovers that New England is Arcadian precisely in its "not bearing the burden of too much history" (14). Arcadia, as Leo Marx reminds us, is "a middle ground, somewhere 'between,' yet in transcendent relation to, the opposing forces of civilization and nature" (23). In describing the middle ground of Chocorua, James is analyzing how civilization has affected America as a whole. If New England is free of a heavy historical burden, the rest of the country must be even more so.

This New England pastoral is marked by the human history that Cole predicted for his own "secluded valley." James reads in the abandoned farms the record of human failure: "scenes of old, hard New England effort, defeated by the soil and the climate and reclaimed by nature and time" (14). He protests mildly that these scenes from the past "interfere" with his present vision of nature ("the mere idleness of the undiscriminated, tangled actual" [15]), but it is clear that the traces of human activity attract him, for in the midst of his complaint

Fig. 9. Thomas Cole, Expulsion from the Garden of Eden, c. 1827–28. Courtesy of Museum of Fine Arts, Boston; gift of Mrs. Maxim Karolik for the Karolik Collection of American Paintings, 1815–65

he anthropomorphizes Chocorua (it "carries its grey head quite with the grandest air" [15]), and goes on to characterize autumn as "a young bedizened, a slightly melodramatic mother" (16) and the scene itself as a "drawing-room" (16). The move from nature toward culture is almost immediate—faced with an empty landscape, James turns to man.[46] In fact, James's New England garden, a timeless paradise, "a stillness exquisite" where "the leaves of the forest turned, one by one, to crimson and to gold, but never broke off" (15), *awaits* the dawn of human history. It is "a stage set" (15), a history of things that "wouldn't, after all, happen: more the pity for them, and for me and for you" (16). In Cole's *Expulsion from the Garden of Eden*, the paradise that is lost and longed for is, as Bryan Jay Wolf says, "a world without history, which dwells instead in its own eternal stasis. There is no past distinguishable from the present, no future different from the past" (94).[47] Only after the Fall does man move into history. But a timeless natural paradise arouses pity in James, pity for the actors and events of history. James longs for the Fall into history because only in time is narrative possible. So strong is James's need to narrate that this picture of a nature safe from civilization moves him to create his own human history. The maples become daughters of noble houses, surrounded by a family of duller trees, waters develop faces, and pines become eyebrows. For all of James's delight in the natural landscape (he has just left a New York that he found shocking in its "squalor" and a New Jersey marked by its "crudity of wealth"), he seems eager to populate and furnish it with his art. Indeed, in the midst of describing his turn from the civilized "human history of places" to natural "commonest objects," James describes "scattered wild apples" as "figures in the carpet" of the landscape (16)!

James inscribes not only his narrative art, but a narrative of himself as artist into the natural landscape before him.[48] However, as James's story "The Figure in the Carpet" hints, this figure cannot be separated out of the landscape and read as its cause or meaning. The carpet *is*, precisely, its textured pattern. The apples in this visually worked landscape point us neither to a final, human explanation for the "undiscriminated, tangled actual" American scene, nor to some natural cause that lies behind James's *American Scene*. The landscape is not the point of origin for James's visual and verbal art; James's art is not the source of the landscape's meaning. The fall into history, into narrative, is also the fall into textuality.

What the figure of the apples does embody is the pattern of history that entwines the natural and the human in James's landscape:

> The apples are everywhere and every interval, every old clearing, an orchard; they have "run down" from neglect and shrunken from cheapness—you pick them up from under your feet but to bite into them, for fellowship, and throw them away; but as you catch their young brightness in the blue air, where they suggest strings of strange-coloured pearls tangled in the knotted boughs, as you note their manner of swarming for a brief and wasted gaiety, they seem to ask to be praised only by the cheerful shepherd and the oaten pipe. (17)

The landscape is one of decay and beauty, "run down" because of man's neglect. James attempts to remedy this neglect—picking up, biting into, and thus using, the apple. This physical use of the landscape seems to open the way for an aesthetic one. Joining in the shepherd's song of praise, James images the apples as pearls ornamenting the hair of the trees.[49] In eating the fruit, James falls into knowledge of an artistic "fellowship" that allows him to see

> a situation interfused with every properest item of sunset and evening star, of darkening circle of forest, of boat that, across the water, put noiselessly out—of analogy, in

short, with every typical triumph of the American landscape "school," now as rococo as so many squares of
ingenious wool-work, but the remembered delight of our
childhood. . . . . That boat across the water is safe, is sus-
taining as far as it goes; it puts out from the cove of
romance, from the inlet of poetry, and glides straight
over, with muffled oar, to the—well, to the right place.
(18) (figs. 10 and 11)

By following the boat deep into the landscape, James's eye
moves back in time. Because the past is present, the landscape
can be literary and the traveler can wind up in the undesignated
"right place." A clue to James's—and America's—destination
lies in the means of transportation: the boat propelled by an
oddly "muffled" oar. Of course, the oar must be muffled if the
boat is to glide "noiselessly," but why mention an oar at all?
The oar points to occupant and action, human history, James's
own story, the stuff of narrative. The oar's presence takes on
added significance when regarded in light of Cole's *Voyage of
Life* series (fig. 12), which represents the pattern of human
history as scenes in the life of the individual. Cole's traveler
has no oar; he passively undergoes the inevitable cycle of history. In James's landscape, where the history of America is
also traced in the travels of an individual, human action remains a possibility.

But the muffled oar also suggests a funeral barge, a reminder
of those fallen apples that figure the American landscape. With
the commencement of human history, the leaf falls from the
tree, things do, "after all, happen," and death and failure become possible. The scene at Chocorua, where "everywhere
legible was the hard little historic record of agricultural failure
and defeat" (21), hints that American civilization may end, as
Cole's *Course of Empire* does, in *Desolation*. The threat that
such an American history poses to James himself is contained
in the muffled oar's uncanny echo of Cole's "traveller who
sees the place at rest close at hand." *Et in Arcadia Ego*.[50] Eating

Fig. 10. Thomas Worthington Whittredge, The Old Hunting Grounds, *1864. Courtesy of Reynolda House Museum of American Art, Winston-Salem, North Carolina*

Fig. 11. Thomas Doughty, Rowing on a Mountain Lake, c. 1835. Courtesy of Hood Museum of Art, Dartmouth College, Hanover, New Hampshire; purchased through the Julia L. Whittier Fund

Fig. 12. Thomas Cole, The Voyage of Life: Manhood, 1840. Courtesy of Munson-Williams-Proctor Institute Museum of Art, Utica, New York

the apple, acknowledging his own transience, James recognizes that his ability to retain a historical American identity rests on his countrymen's capacity to preserve a historical American countryside. Only if Americans respond to what James calls "the touching appeal of nature" will desolation be avoided: "The 'Do something kind for me,' is not so much a 'Live upon me and thrive by me' as a 'Live *with* me, somehow, and let us make out together what we may do for each other—something that is not merely estimable in more or less greasy greenbacks.... See how I lend myself to poetry and sociability—positively to aesthetic use: give me that consolation' " (21). Seeing the apples as pearls, watching the boat's progress into the center of the landscape, James has answered this appeal by putting America to aesthetic use. Neither detached nor distant, Jamesian aesthetic perception represents an active, deep engagement with what is seen.

Yet, throughout most of *The American Scene* such visual engagement proves impossible. The book's final episode powerfully illustrates James's dilemma. Riding in a Pullman car, James hears the train's rhythm invite him (" 'See what I'm making of all this—see what I'm making, what I'm making!' " [463]) to answer his Arcadian question: Can Americans live "with," not "upon" the land? James's enraged response—" 'I see what you are *not* making, oh, what you are ever so vividly not' " (463)—is not a call for an earlier, uncivilized America.[51] Unlike the "painted savages" whom the railroad has dispossessed or "some tough reactionary" (463), James's values are not purely natural; he accepts, as Cole did, civilization's price. The Arcadian landscape's plea that Americans and America "make out together what we may do for each other" is a call for a cooperation—a middle ground—between nature and culture. However, America has given up nature without getting culture in return. Topography, local detail, history, and meaning all disappear as the landscape becomes quantified into an

undifferentiated series of "stops": "You shall multiply the per-
petrations you call 'places'—by the sign of some name as sense-
less, mostly, as themselves—to the sole end of multiplying to
the eye, as one approaches, every possible source of displea-
sure" (464). Nothing halts the railroad; all is equal before it—
or rather beneath it. James finds himself groaning for "a split
or a chasm . . . an unbridgeable abyss or an insuperable mountain" (465), anything that would force a distinction and stop
the flat "criminal continuity" of the railroad. What most
Americans praised—the railroad's "annihilation of space and
time"—is what enrages James.[52] His fears for the future are
not allayed by the traditional American reply to the European
spectator who finds the New World landscape lacking in history. "The moral feeling with which a man of sentiment and
knowledge looks upon the plains of your hemisphere, is con-
nected with his recollections; here it should be mingled with
his hopes," Cooper's John Cadwallader tells the Count de—
in *Notions of the Americans* (1828).[53] James's landscapes, created
nearly eighty years later by a Europeanized American spectator,
show that looking always to the future means ignoring the
present and erasing the past.

Yet locating the source of James's rage here does not explain
its uncontrolled expression, unique in *The American Scene*. The
explanation lies in James's own historicity, his complicity with
American progress, and is marked, as it was on the Hazy Hudson, by his position in the scene. James occupies and, as Holland observes, is identified with the ravaging Pullman car
(433).[54] Seated beside the "plate-glass" window—that invention essential to tourism and consumerism, to observation cars
and department stores—James consumes the landscape as he
speeds across it.[55] Early in *The Ambassadors*, Strether focuses
on the plate-glass that protects him from direct engagement
with the pleasures of Paris; *The American Scene* places such
perceptions in their cultural context. James's window view is,

as he confessed earlier in South Carolina, a bought privilege: "the spectator enjoying from his supreme seat of ease his extraordinary, his awful modern privilege of this detached yet concentrated stare at the misery of subject populations. (Subject, I mean, to this superiority of his bought convenience—subject even as never, of old, to the sway of satraps or proconsuls)" (397–98).

James, like Ruskin before him, exposes the dark side of the picturesque spectator who, standing at a distance, views only the surface of the landscape.[56] As railroad traveler, James is literally living "upon" the land, viewing its population with the imperial gaze of power. In "The Consuming Vision of Henry James," Jean-Christophe Agnew analyzes the role of "mental consumption" in the late nineteenth-century rise of consumer culture, delineating "a way of seeing" that is "visually acquisitive." Agnew argues that "for every actual purchase, countless contemplated purchases prepare the way. A habit of mind thus develops that uses the commodity without, in the conventional sense, using it up."[57] Such, James implies, is the railroad traveler's view of America. The spectator's very distance from the scene, his inability to use it humanly, is not protective but destructive. Earlier able to walk about Arcadia's middle ground, eating apples and seeing them as figures in the carpet or pearls adorning humanized trees, James is now inhumanly detached from the countryside that, ironically, he scans for "the germ of anything finely human, of anything agreeably or successfully social" (465).

The "germ" of the human is, as we know from the Prefaces, the source of narrative. These are the years when James's literary imagination returns to America.[58] But while he finds America a fit subject for reviewing his youth or for writing short stories about encounters between the past and the present, a full-scale fiction of contemporary American life proves impossible for James. The ending of *The American Scene* shows us why. Because James cannot finally locate himself in this landscape, he will turn away from writing about it. Despite repeated attempts to use the visual strategies of his childhood to place himself in America, James ends by perceiving the American scene as a twentieth-century American. The disconcerting final picture of *The American Scene* shows James viewing the landscape not as a calm European tourist with no emotional stake in what is seen, but as an angry American who participates despite himself in the very progress that serves to dislocate him.[59] Perceiving a landscape historically means that, rather than a fixed self regarding a completed past, a changing presence sees a changing present. If James starts his perceptual journey as Rip Van Winkle, he ends as Ichabod Crane: the alien figure of a traveler en route to somewhere else, visually commodifying and consuming the landscape as he goes. In 1819 Irving can preserve a place for the American narrative imagination by making Ichabod a solitary grotesque outcast from the comfortable, settled community that nestles in Sleepy Hollow.[60] But by 1904, *The American Scene* shows that "we are all tourists now."[61] James's profoundly American discomfort at the end of *The American Scene* sets the stage for an act that reveals how seriously he regarded the question of national identity: the renunciation of his citizenship. Like the painters who included ax, train, and figure in their landscapes, James traces the coming destruction of an American identity in the landscape of *The American Scene*.

Notes

1. See "Sunnyside: The Provincial Background," in David L. Furth's *The Visionary Betrayed: Aesthetic Discontinuity in Henry James's The American Scene* (Cambridge: Harvard University Press, 1979), 9–22.

2. Letter to Mrs. Francis Child quoted in Peter Buitenhuis's *The Grasping Imagination: The American Writings of Henry James* (Toronto: University of Toronto Press, 1970), 180.

3. The scene's mixture of familiarity and strangeness results, at least in part, from the fact that James had gone on a week's walking tour in the White Mountains in 1861 and climbed Mount Washington. Thus, whether or not this is his first view of Chocorua, the scene is not new.

4. Judith Fetterley, *The Resisting Reader: A Feminist Approach to American Fiction* (Bloomington: Indiana University Press, 1978), 9.

5. The New England chapters in particular have been seen as nostalgic. For example, see William F. Hall, "The Continuing Relevance of Henry James' 'The American Scene,' " *Criticism* 13 (Spring 1971): 151–65.

6. Alan Trachtenberg, "The American Scene: Versions of the City," *Massachusetts Review* 8 (Spring 1967): 294. See also Gordon O. Taylor's treatment of *The American Scene* as autobiography, "Chapters of Experience: *The American Scene*," *Genre* 12 (Spring 1979): 93–116.

7. John Barrell, *The Idea of Landscape and the Sense of Place, 1730–1840: An Approach to the Poetry of John Clare* (Cambridge: Cambridge University Press, 1972).

8. Cf. Richard A. Hocks, *Henry James and Pragmatistic Thought* (Chapel Hill: University of North Carolina Press, 1974): "One can see nevertheless why the mentality which truly embodies William's pluralism would become more and more drawn to little things, tiny matters. Nothing is ever finished in the usual sense, the smallest matter yielding almost unlimited possibilities of meaning" (92).

9. Roger B. Stein, *John Ruskin and Aesthetic Thought in America, 1840–1900* (Cambridge: Harvard University Press, 1967), ix.

10. See Stein, "Ruskinism in America: *The Crayon* (1855–61)," in *John Ruskin and Aesthetic Thought*, 101–23.

11. See Viola Hopkins Winner's discussion of Ruskin's influence on James, *Henry James and the Visual Arts* (Charlottesville: University of Virginia Press, 1970), 18–28, as well as James's 20 March 1869 letter to his mother describing dinner at Ruskin's (1:102–5).

12. Winner, *Henry James and the Visual Arts*, 28, 19.

13. Elizabeth Helsinger, *Ruskin and the Art of the Beholder* (Cambridge: Harvard University Press, 1982). The discussion that follows draws on Helsinger's "The Romantic Reader and the Visual Arts," 167–200.

14. Ibid , 181.

15. Furth, *The Visionary Betrayed*, 16. What James abhors here is much like what R. W. B. Lewis calls the doctrine of "the sovereign

present" in "The Case against the Past," in *The American Adam: Innocence, Tragedy, and Tradition in the Nineteenth Century* (Chicago: University of Chicago Press, 1955), 13–27.

16. Both writers show their desire to read architecture by wishing that houses had commemorative tablets or stones to tell the history of their inhabitants.

17. John Carlos Rowe: "The 'vanished . . . birthplace,' that Washington Place house where Henry was born in 1843, sets the tone for all the other historical absences he encounters in *The American Scene*" (*The Theoretical Dimensions of Henry James* [Madison: University of Wisconsin Press, 1984], 214).

18. James also describes this flattening out of the landscape into a monotonous equality as a "whitewash," a choice of metaphor that has its source both in the actual American practice of painting houses white and in the traditional picturesque abhorrence of white paint. On whitewash, see James T. Callow, *Kindred Spirits: Knickerbocker Writers and American Artists, 1807–1855* (Chapel Hill: The University of North Carolina Press, 1967), 204–7, and Blake Nevius, *Cooper's Landscapes: An Essay on the Picturesque Vision* (Berkeley: University of California Press, 1976), 58–59.

19. On textiles and textuality, see Roland Barthes, *The Pleasure of the Text*, trans. Richard Howard (New York: Hill and Wang, 1975).

20. However, James's and the Hudson River painters' use of near-looking detail is opposite in technique to the "full but indistinct space" that Ruskin praises in Turner's blurred foregrounds.

21. Asher Durand, "Letters on Landscape Painting, No. 3," *The Crayon* 1, 31 January 1855, 66. Both *The Crayon* in general and Durand's *Letters* in particular were extremely influential with American artists and critics.

22. Asher Durand, "Letters on Landscape Painting, No. 5," *The Crayon* 1, 7 March 1855, 146.

23. Barbara Novak, *American Painting of the Nineteenth Century: Realism, Idealism, and the American Experience*, 2nd ed. (New York: Harper and Row, 1979), 240.

24. The latter characterization of James's vision is taken from Winner, *Henry James and the Visual Arts*, 32.

25. Karl Kroeber, *Romantic Landscape Vision: Constable and Wordsworth* (Madison: University of Wisconsin Press, 1975), 73.

26. See Novak's essays on Thomas Cole and Asher Durand in *American Painting*, 61–79; 80–91.

27. "Man's Traces: Axe, Train, Figure" is the title of Chapter 8 of Novak's *Nature and Culture: American Landscape Painting, 1825–1875* (New York: Oxford University Press, 1980), 157–200. Novak discusses the Durand painting on pages 172–73. Inness's *The Lackawanna Valley* is another, if more ambiguous, example of this phenomenon. On literary attempts to create a similar continuity, see Donald A. Ringe, *The Pictorial Mode: Space and Time in the Art of Bryant, Irving and Cooper* (Lexington: University of Kentucky Press, 1971), 164–204, and Robert A. Ferguson's "William Cullen Bryant: The Creative Context of the Poet," *New England Quarterly* 53 (December 1980): 431–63, which analyzes Bryant's need to control both nature and his response to it in context of American associationist aesthetics.

28. Winner, *Henry James and the Visual Arts*, 25. In her astute, but unfortunately quite short, discussion of this point, Winner also compares James to Irving.

29. See, for example, *Principles*, 1:228–29, where William James describes brain changes as resembling the aurora borealis. That Henry James thinks of iridescence as three-dimensional is made clear by the Preface to "Daisy Miller," where he describes "the surface iridescent, even in the short piece, by what is beneath it and what throbs and gleams through" (*AN*, 278). See also James's repeated descriptions of the historical Italian landscape as "iridescent" in *Italian Hours* (1909).

30. "An array of modern 'impressionistic' pictures, mainly French, wondrous examples of Manet, of Degas, of Claude Monet, of Whistler, of other rare recent hands, treated us to the momentary effect of a large slippery sweet inserted, without a warning, between the compressed lips of half-conscious inanition" (45–46).

31. Although modern art critics would characterize this flat landscape as more "postimpressionist" than "impressionist," James would not have recognized the distinction. He classes Whistler, whose Japanese-influenced seascapes this Cape Cod scene resembles, along with Manet, Degas, and Monet, as " 'impressionistic' " (45–46). On James and postimpressionism, see Winner, *Henry James and the Visual Arts*, 53. Buitenhuis, *The Grasping Imagination*, 184–85, argues that James uses a predominantly impressionist model in *The American Scene*. However, while James praises such paintings, they simply do not serve his needs in describing the American landscape. I cannot list here all the scholarship on James and "literary impressionism," but

recent contributions include H. Peter Stowell, *Literary Impressionism, James and Chekhov* (Athens: University of Georgia Press, 1980); James Kirschke, *Henry James and Impressionism* (Troy, N.Y.: Whitston Publishing, 1981); and Rowe, "Phenomenological Hermeneutics: Henry James and Literary Impressionism," in *The Theoretical Dimensions*, 189–217.

32. Although I disagree with his equation of the visual with the ahistorical purity and "sheer surface" (*The Theoretical Dimensions*, 204) of the "literary impression," Rowe captures James's problem here: "The 'restless analyst' seems to encounter in travel the sheer scenic experience in which people figure as monuments and artifacts in the service of impressions. . . . Insofar as observation refuses to 'go behind' the object of sense, then the closed form (the monument or objet d'art) seems to deny its history, cancel its temporality, and block the viewer's 'entrance' " (*The Theoretical Dimensions*, 202).

33. On nineteenth-century literary treatments of the railroad's effect on the American landscape, see Leo Marx, *The Machine in the Garden: Technology and the Pastoral Ideal in America* (New York: Oxford University Press, 1964). Using the railroad's intrusion into Farmington, Connecticut, as his example, Marx argues briefly that the machine conquers the Arcadian garden in *The American Scene*.

34. See Rowe, *The Theoretical Dimensions*, 212–17, on the suppression of the Civil War in James's discussions of the southern cities in *The American Scene*.

35. Joshua Taylor explores these two points of view in "Europe and the Great Tradition" and "The Identification of Art with America" in *The Fine Arts in America* (Chicago: University of Chicago Press, 1979), 52–65; 65–89. That James does not wish to make his native land into Europe does not, of course, mean that he never judges America by European standards. See Furth, "The Squire and the Parson: The European Background," in *The Visionary Betrayed*, 23–35.

36. James also manages to see such Hudson River landscapes elsewhere in America: see, for example, his descriptions of both a Maryland country club and the nearby Carroll house (328–31). In using a deep, full, detailed pictorial space for his historical compositions James draws on what Stephen Bann, in "The Sense of the Past: Image, Text, and Object in the Formation of Historical Consciousness in Nineteenth-Century Britain," in *The New Historicism*, ed. H. Aram Veeser (New York: Routledge, 1989), describes as the three primary

rhetorical techniques employed in successful nineteenth-century representations of the past: "*Framing* is concerned with the physical operation of delimiting an area and designating it as authentic; *focalizing* is concerned with identifying objects of special interest within that area, and in that way contributing to the authenticity of the whole; *filling* . . . is the final operation of establishing the otherness of history not simply as a visual or verbal system of references but as a perceived or imagined fullness—no less concrete than the everyday world" (105–6). See also Bann's brief discussion of James's *The Sense of the Past* (115).

37. Novak, *Nature and Culture*, 184.

38. Even the failed impressionist picture had its verandahed bungalow (significantly, in this scene where history remains largely absent, the dwelling stays peripheral). Cities, the clearest records of American civilization, are also, for James, evidence of that civilization's failure. Philadelphia, suffused with Franklin's presence, is the exception; however, even Philadelphia also has its dark side, as Mark Seltzer shows in *Henry James and the Art of Power* (Ithaca: Cornell University Press, 1984), 115–25.

39. See Rowe, "For both Hawthorne and James, the American fall is characterized by the modern loss of the past and willful repudiation of tradition as much as it is a consequence of the surrender to the past or of the mere 'lack' of history" (*The Theoretical Dimensions*, 33).

40. James continues, "It is of the essence of the land, in these regions, to throw you back, after a little, upon the possible humanities, so it often results from social study, too baffling in many a case, that you are thrown back upon the land. That agreeable, if sometimes bewildering, seesaw is perhaps the best figure, in such conditions, for the restless analyst's tenor of life" (43).

41. See Novak's aptly titled essay, "Thomas Cole: The Dilemma of the Real and the Ideal," in *American Painting*, 61–79.

42. Thomas Cole, "Essay on American Scenery," *The American Monthly Magazine*, n.s., 1 (January 1836), in *American Art, 1700–1960: Sources and Documents*, ed. John W. McCoubrey (Englewood Cliffs, N.J.: Prentice-Hall, 1965), 98–110. All subsequent quotations will be taken from this edition and will be given in the text.

43. *New York Mirror*, 22 October 1856, 135, quoted in Novak, *American Painting*, 69.

44. In his use of Venice, James echoes both Ruskin's *Stones of Venice* (1851–53), vols. 9–11 of *Complete Works*, and Cooper's *The Bravo* (1831). On the tradition of the American New Earth, see Cecelia Tichi, *New World, New Earth: Environmental Reform in American Literature from the Puritans through Whitman* (New Haven: Yale University Press, 1979).

45. Bryan Jay Wolf, *Romantic Re-Vision: Culture and Consciousness in Nineteenth-Century American Painting and Literature* (Chicago: University of Chicago Press, 1982), 91–101.

46. This interest in the humanized middle ground accords with James's marked disinterest in the sublime aspects of the American scenery. During *The American Scene* trip he fails to visit that icon of American sublimity, Niagara Falls, and the sequel to *The American Scene*, which was to deal with the American West, was never written. James did visit Niagara in 1871, a trip that he described in two short articles that stressed the falls' *"pleasing"* qualities over their sublimity: "The pure beauty of elegance and grace is the grand characteristic of the Fall. It is not in the least monstrous" ("Niagara 1 & 2," *The Nation*, 12 and 19 October 1871, 238–39 and 254–55).

47. The painting and its connection to narrative are also discussed in Bryan Jay Wolf's "A Grammar of the Sublime, or Intertextuality Triumphant in Church, Turner, and Cole," *New Literary History* 16 (Winter 1985): 329–32.

48. For an essay that "interpret[s] James's America in the light of James's act of representing it in *The American Scene*" (412), see Laurence Holland's "Representation and Renewal in Henry James's *The American Scene*," in *The Expense of Vision: Essays on the Craft of Henry James* (1964; reprint, Baltimore: John Hopkins University Press, 1982), 411–34. "The Figure in the Carpet" has been widely read as a Jamesian allegory of authorship. See, for example, Tzvetan Todorov, "The Secret of Narrative," in *The Poetics of Prose*, trans. Richard Howard (Ithaca: Cornell University Press, 1977), 143–78, and Wolfgang Iser, *The Act of Reading: A Theory of Aesthetic Response* (Baltimore: Johns Hopkins University Press, 1978), 3-10.

49. Added evidence that this use of nature is both aesthetic and Jamesian is the fact that Vereker, the artist in "The Figure in the Carpet," describes the figure as "the very string . . . that my pearls are strung on!" (*The Complete Tales of Henry James*, ed. Leon Edel, 12 vols. [Philadelphia: J. B. Lippincott, 1961–64], 9:289). In *The American Scene* James also uses this image to describe the New Jersey shore

villas (7). Robert Gale, *The Caught Image: Figurative Language in the Fiction of Henry James* (Chapel Hill: University of North Carolina Press, 1964), notes James's use of pearls "in descriptions of artistic work" (188).

50. See Erwin Panofsky, "*Et in Arcadia Ego*: Poussin and the Elegiac Tradition," in *Meaning in the Visual Arts* (1955; reprint, Chicago: University of Chicago Press, 1982), 295–320. It is unclear whether James knew what Panofsky has shown to be the correct translation of the phrase: "Death is even in Arcadia." James uses the words in their modern (until Panofsky) sense of "I, too, was born, or lived in Arcady" in "Brooksmith" (1891). See also Rowe, *The Theoretical Dimensions*, who argues that nature, not history, signals man's mortality: "The very air of nature exhales the death/negation of man that prompts his curious defenses in the construction of cities, the invention of language and the illusion of history" (201).

51. Holland, *The Expense of Vision*, 432–33. Holland notes that Wright Morris, *The Territory Ahead: Critical Interpretations in American Literature* (New York: Harcourt, Brace, 1958), 112, 210–11, also sees James as committed to the future here.

52. The phrase is from Marx, *The Machine in the Garden*, 194.

53. James Fenimore Cooper, *Notions of the Americans: Picked up by a Travelling Bachelor* (1828), quoted in Nevius, *Cooper's Landscapes*, 23–24. Nevius goes on to show that Cooper (like his fellow traveling bachelor James) grew dissatisfied with this position after visiting Europe.

54. For a study that uncovers a different Jamesian complicity by revealing " 'criminal continuity' between the techniques of representation that the novelist devises and the technologies of power that his fiction ostensibly censors and disavows" (14), see Mark Seltzer, "Advertising America: *The American Scene*," in *Henry James and the Art of Power*, 96–145.

55. On the relationship between plate glass and consumerism, see Daniel Boorstin, *The Americans: The Democratic Experience* (New York: Random House, 1973), 103–4, 336–45, and Rachel Bowlby, *Just Looking: Consumer Culture in Dreiser, Gissing and Zola* (New York: Methuen, 1985).

56. Ruskin's major critique of the picturesque is in *Modern Painters IV*, vol. 6. of *Complete Works*. See also Rowe's analysis of Jamesian tourism, *The Theoretical Dimensions*, 194–204.

57. Jean-Christophe Agnew, "The Consuming Vision of Henry James," in *The Culture of Consumption: Critical Essays in American History, 1880–1980,* ed. Richard Wightman Fox and T. J. Jackson Lears (New York: Pantheon Books, 1983), 73.

58. See, for example, his letter to William James on 24 May 1903 (4:270–76).

59. See Walter Benn Michaels, *The Gold Standard and the Logic of Naturalism* (Berkeley: University of California Press, 1987): "Although transcending your origins in order to evaluate them has been the opening move in cultural criticism at least since Jeremiah, it is surely a mistake to take this move at face value: not so much because you can't really transcend your culture but because, if you could, you wouldn't have any terms of evaluation left—except, perhaps, theological ones" (18).

60. Of course, even in 1819, Irving makes it clear that such havens for the imagination are fast disappearing in America.

61. So Barrell concludes his study of Clare, *The Idea of Landscape,* 188.

CHAPTER 4

The Architecture of the Jamesian Eye

Home as Seen

JAMES'S FINAL LOSS—or refusal—of an American identity has its counterpart in his creation of an English self. His perceptions of the American landscape reveal James's unsuccessful attempt to retain a connection with an earlier time; his visual pictures of England illustrate a historical consistency that is at once national and personal. Nonetheless, precisely because it is historical—a changing presence's interaction with a changing present—this consistency is constantly threatened with disruption. The fall into history that *The American Scene* documents brings with it the threat of dissolution. Seeing England, James seeks to avoid the chaotic abyss of twentieth-century history where change is constant and random, where identities cannot hold, by focusing on visible structures.

The self that James works to see in the English landscape is fundamentally literary. Henry James's writing is an essential part of what William James calls "*the material Self*" (1:280). "There are few men who would not feel personally annihilated if a life-long construction of their hands or brains—say an entomological collection or an extensive work in manuscript— were suddenly swept away" (1:281). Henry's texts are so "saturated with [his] . . . labor" that he *is* his writing (1:281). This literary identity is located in others and over time. As in *The Golden Bowl*, "the true, the intimate, the ultimate, the permanent Me which I seek" is that potential "ideal social self . . . a self that is at least *worthy* of approving recognition by the highest *possible* judging companion" (*Principles*, 1:301). Maggie is finally fixed by the fact that she is left with her limited husband as that highest companion; for Henry the judge is literary posterity—the community of readers who will read and value his writing after he is gone. Contrary to the critical image of an aloof, aristocratic Master, isolated from his world, James's English landscape portraits display a self that is profoundly social.

The English place where this "Henry James" is most firmly located is James's self-created home: East Sussex. This chapter will focus on two essays, one written three years before and the other ten years after *The American Scene*, in which James endeavors, under differing historical conditions, to picture a habitable landscape for himself. In his 1901 "Winchelsea, Rye, and 'Denis Duval,' " visual exploration of the landscape of East Sussex provides James with the opportunity to investigate the contingent nature of his identity as a writer—dependent upon readers and subject to time. James's East Sussex pictures are centered on Lamb House, the architectural structure that embodies his writing self, and they serve as the terms for his perceptual analysis of that self. Strolling into and about Winchelsea and Rye, meditating on Thackeray's unfinished novel, James stands in a series of double positions: the writer who is a reader, the present perceiver who looks for visible traces of the past, and the adult who tries to maintain identity with his youth. The process of representation is literally foregrounded in this essay as James pictures both the site of painting and the scene of writing.

In *The American Scene* James rejected static, flat, inhuman, and ahistorical landscapes in favor of a deep visual space marked by temporal traces and personal narrative. By 1914, when historical perceptions seem unattainable even in England, James turns to a visual investigation of·the "givens" that governed such scenes. The depth that James perceives as historicity is shown to be the space, not only of narration, but also of signification.

James describes himself as pacing the heights of Rye, barely "Within the Rim" of civilization and history, looking alternately out across the English Channel to Belgium and back into the English landscape. His perception of the blank curve of the horizon discomposes his familiar picture of his English home. This "shock of events" is such that the identities of both "England" and "Henry James" are threatened. His perceptual habits broken, James is forced, like Maggie in *The Golden Bowl*, into self-conscious revision—he must visually reconstruct the English landscape in order to reidentify himself. Attempting to maintain continuity while incorporating change, James uncovers the narrative nature of identity. Visually plotting England's boundaries, James endeavors to weave an account of his self. What he recognizes is that this narrative of identity is historical both in its making and in its medium. Exploring the temporal contextuality of his visual images and the constructed textuality of his own identity, James confronts the historicity of language. For James, the events of 1914 underscore the fact that words *"show* as signifying" only "in the circumstances."

"Winchelsea, Rye, and 'Denis Duval' "

I delight in a palpable imaginable *visitable* past—in the nearer distances and the clearer mysteries, the marks and

> signs of a world we may reach over to as by making a
> long arm we grasp an object at the other end of our own
> table.... With more moves back the element of the
> appreciable shrinks—just as the charm of looking over a
> garden-wall into another garden breaks down when
> successions of walls appear. (*AN*, 164)

Generally read as a sign of James's disinterest in all but the
most recent history, what this much-quoted passage from the
Preface to *The Aspern Papers* actually describes is the present's
physical connection with the past. Because it endures materially into the present, recent history is "palpable." James participates here in what Stephen Bann has called the nineteenth
century's "rhetoric of evocation," wherein "the senses are in-
veigled into an act of identification with the otherness of the
past."[1] The Preface's metaphoric discussion of space as time is
literalized in the landscape of "Winchelsea, Rye, and 'Denis
Duval.'" James finds that while he cannot "place" or " 'vis-
ualise' " the great battles that constitute the towns' usual claims
to history, "what I do see, on the other hand, very comfortably,
is the little undistinguished picture of a nearer antiquity, the
antiquity for a glimpse of which I reopened 'Denis Duval' "
(175). This nearer and clearer past is "visitable," not only by
the imagination, but also by the body; it is not too far away
to walk. The penetrable landscape of East Sussex fosters the
excursive perception so difficult to achieve in America. History
becomes familiar, domestic: all we need do is "reach over as
by making a long arm we grasp an object at the other end of
our own table" or look over the garden wall. The physical
counterparts for this temporal table and garden, located at
Lamb House, are the foci of James's excursive visual explorations of his historical self in "Winchelsea, Rye, and 'Denis
Duval.' "

The past's presence is so immediate in Winchelsea that
James describes the region as "haunted" with history. By

showing the traces of its lost past, Winchelsea activates the eye of the viewer: "If I spoke just now of Winchelsea as haunted, let this somewhat overworked word stand as an ineffectual tribute to the small, sad, civic history that the place appeals to us to reconstruct as we gaze vaguely about" (169). The appeal to "reconstruct" is not a call for architectural restoration, a practice that James, following Ruskin, vehemently opposes.[2] Despite its ostensible respect for the past, the English practice of restoring buildings actually resembles the American one of razing them. Both actions falsify history by erasing the marks of time.

Instead, James calls for visual reconstruction. Such perceptual activity is fostered by the fact that Winchelsea is a fragment filled with fragments. The first Winchelsea is "drowned"; the next is left "high and dry"; the unfinished thirteenth-century city lies in ruins; church, streets, and city-wall are all incomplete: "the noble fragment of her great church, rising solid from the abortive symmetry of her great square"; "abstract avenues and cross-streets straggle away, through the summer twilight, into mere legend and mystery"; the "old vague girdle is lost to-day in the fields where the sheep browse"(171). Like the novel set there, this landscape intrigues because it is broken. As James says of the unfinished *Denis Duval*: "If, moreover, it after a few months broke short off, that really gave it something as well as took something away" (163). Literary and landscape fragments interest James because they demand, and leave room for, his response.[3] The town's "sense of obliterated history" means that "the air is like that of a room through which something has been carried that you are aware of without having seen it" (177). What William James says of perception in general—"*Whilst part of what we perceive comes through our senses from the object before us, another part* (and it may be the larger part) *always comes . . . out of our own head*" (2:747)—holds especially true for incomplete or broken structures. Strether visually fills in the inscriptions on the medals and books in Marie de Vionnet's apartment; James, as both writer and perceiver, is attracted to unfinished forms that allow his active engagement. Written in an architectural and topographical palimpsest, Winchelsea's history invites reading.

Yet, as *The American Scene* illustrates, to enter the world of historical narrative is to run the risk of a fall. James, along with other observers of ruins since the eighteenth century, reads them as signs of the futility of human work in the face of time.[4] Wandering among Winchelsea's ruins, James sees them as evidence that the town "had only time to dream a great dream—the dream of a scant pair of centuries—before its hopes were turned to bitterness and its boasts to lamentation" (170). The writer's death may leave his works unfinished,[5] or even his finished texts to ruin. James's description of the New York Edition in the year before his death displays his fear: "my poor old rather truncated edition, in fact entirely frustrated one—which has the grotesque likeness for me of a sort of miniature Ozymandias of Egypt ('look on my *works*, ye mighty, and despair!')—round which the lone and level sands stretch further away than ever."[6] After death, manuscripts, monuments, and memories are the self.[7] Like Ruskin, James couples poetry and architecture as the "two strong conquerors of the forgetfulness of men" (Ruskin, 8:224), but, like Ruskin too, he fears that in "the age of loss" modern man may have lost the ability to remember (8:246). If the New York Edition is forgotten the way the house at Ashburton Place was, if James's "poetry" is, in effect, erased the way his "architecture" has been, he will disappear from history. His course will be that of Cole's Empire.[8] It is this need to survive over time, this search for a community of readers, that propels James's perceptual excursions into the English countryside.

Rereading Thackeray in 1901 is a "literary adventure" for James because in doing so he is attempting to scan his own literary future (162). The unpredictability of the rereading adventure lies in the fact that, as William James explains, "Experience is remoulding us every moment" (1:228). If experience is constantly changing us, the self that rereads a book is not the same as the self that originally read it. How, then, can the past survive into the present, how can we be loyal to the books of long ago? William James explains that the stream of thought is "a slow shifting in which there is always some common ingredient retained. The commonest element of all, the most uniform, is the possession of the same memories" (1:352). For Henry James, readerly loyalty depends upon this ability to remember. Since he regards the experience of reading itself as social and personal, he claims that what we recall in rereading is our feeling for the author. "The beauty is particularly the beauty of its [*Denis Duval's*] being its author's. . . . Our appreciation changes—how in the world, with experience always battering away, shouldn't it?—but our feeling, more happily, doesn't" (163). Even a loyal reader like James cannot repeat the past. However, as Strether's visual example shows, James can allow his feelings to direct his attentive selection of associations. Such efforts to remember are acts of autobiography, as James's description of how Denis Duval tells his own story suggests: "The recital here, as every one remembers, is autobiographic; the old battered, but considerably enriched, world-worn, but finely sharpened Denis looks back upon a troubled life from the winter fireside and places you, in his talkative and contagious way—he is a practised literary artist—in possession of the story. We see him in a placid port after many voyages" (163–64). The Denis Duval that James describes is the product of interaction with his environment over time. "Battered" and "worn" by experience, he is nonetheless "enriched" and "sharpened." Created by his past, Duval now turns back to recreate it. Memory is not nostalgic but narrative. In describing Thackeray's Duval, James hints at the autobio-

graphical function of "Winchelsea, Rye, and 'Denis Duval.' "
Like his own characters, in actively remembering, James
chooses a past. Safe in the placid port of Rye, affectionately
recalling his past experiences as a reader, he narrates his self.

Using the words "battering" and "battered" to connect the
lives of narrator and audience, James implies a shared experience. He warns against the dangers of an impersonal, ahistorical reading: "Woe to the mere official critic, the critic who
has never felt the *man*" (163). Although Thackeray may now
exist only in readers like James, past readings of Thackeray
have molded James into his present self.[9] To read without
remembering is therefore to end up alone, isolated both from
intimacy with the author and from one's own past. James's
attempts to avoid such isolation can be traced in his visual
pictures of Winchelsea and Rye. Rather than looking with an
ahistorical eye at the unimportant towns of 1901, James actively
fills out the present scene with memories of the past. What
directs his perceptions is his deep need to maintain the profoundly social relationship whereby reader and author create
and sustain one another over time.[10]

James is, of course, both reader and writer. The duality of
his position in "Winchelsea, Rye, and 'Denis Duval' " is de-
ployed spatially as he wanders, Strether-like, between the two
towns and stands first on one side, and then the other, of the
Lamb House garden wall. However, as we know from the
Preface to *The Golden Bowl*, reader and writer are not fully
separable. Rereading *is* "revision" for James. "Winchelsea,
Rye, and 'Denis Duval' " represents such re-vision literally:
James attempts to ascertain Thackeray's authorial intent by
trying see the landscape as the earlier writer did. "What—in
the light, at least, of later fashions,—the place has to offer the
actual observer is the effect of an object seen, a thing of aspect
and suggestion, situation and colour; but what had it to offer
Thackeray—or the taste of forty years ago—that he so oddly

forbore to give us a tangled clue to? The impression of to-day's reader is that the chapters we possess might really have been written without the author's having stood on the spot" (166). Since James knows that Thackeray had, in fact, seen Winchelsea,[11] he concludes that the explanation for the novel's lack of landscape must lie in the perceptual and literary differences betweeen 1864 and 1901. "The thing is not forty years old, but it points already—and that is above all the amusement of it—to a general *poetic* that, both on its positive and its negative sides, we have left well behind" (167).

Initially, James's position as a twentieth-century writer appears to be that of the naive realist: Thackeray's novel is puzzling because it makes no attempt to hold a mirror up to nature, to render the world of objects out there. However, what the landscape offers James in 1901 is not "an object," but "an object seen"; not an environment, but a relationship between an environment and a perceiver. James's own informed eye sees the potential for perceptual composition in the scene: "a thing of aspect and suggestion, situation and colour."

> It is impossible to stand to-day in the high, loose, sunny, haunted square of Winchelsea without wondering what he could have been thinking of. There are ladies in view with easels, sun-bonnets, and white umbrellas—often perceptibly, too, with nothing else that makes for successful representation; but I doubt if it were these apparitions that took the bloom from his vision, for they were much less frequent in those looser days, and moreover would have formed much more a reason for not touching the place at all than for taking it up indifferently. Of any impulse to make the reader see it with seeing eyes his page, at all events, gives no sign. (168)

James's "square" is a picture of representation. His perceptual analysis of Winchelsea is at once personal and mediated: he looks at the scene through other artists. Just as James's reading of *Denis Duval* focuses on its gaps in representation (the missing ending, the lack of visual description), so, too, Thackeray's absence haunts James's view. Perhaps all too present are contemporary attempts at depiction: the lady painters, whose "easels, sun-bonnets, and white umbrellas"[12] provide light-catching accents for James's composition, have themselves been arranged in the scene by still another set of artists, the painting instructors who "distribute their disciples over the place, at selected points, where the master, going his round from hour to hour, reminds you of nothing so much as a busy *chef* with many saucepans on the stove and periodically lifting their covers for a sniff and a stir" (173).[13]

As he perceives, James analyzes and incorporates previous pictorial strategies. James's revising of Thackeray makes him reader and writer; seeing this landscape, he is both audience and artist.

> The tidal river, on the left, wanders away to Rye Harbour and its bar, where the black fishing-boats, half the time at lop-sided rest in the mud, make a cluster of slanting spears against the sky. When the river is full we are proud of its wide light and many curves; when it is empty we call it, for vague reasons, 'rather Dutch'; and empty or full we sketch it in the fine weather as hard as ever we can. When I say 'we' I mean *they* do—it is to speak with hospitality. They mostly wear, as I have hinted, large sun-bonnets, and they crouch on low camp-stools; they put in, as they would say, a bit of white, in places often the least likely. Rye is in truth a rudimentary drawing-lesson, and you quite embrace the question when you have fairly seized the formula. Nothing so 'quaint' was ever so easy—nothing so easy was ever so quaint. (173)

The shifting personal pronouns ("we," "I," "they," "you") in this passage point to the social, cooperative nature of James's perceptual picture. Rye provides compositional elements that even the beginning painter can recognize and use: the river that leads the eye into the distance; the dark accent of the fishing-boats that supply a convenient set of diagonals and, like a Claudian tree, establish a plane; the shining, flat, curving expanse of water or the darker " 'Dutch' " line around which to compose the scene.

Like James's American Hudson River landscapes, this "quaint," "Dutch" picture of Rye has neither the beauty of a classical scene nor the grandeur of a sublime one. Instead, James composes a perceptual record of intimacy with the land. "Much more to be loved than feared," Rye provides James with a safe visual space in which to explore those aspects of the self that are most threatening (173).

The center of this homely landscape is the house that visibly embodies James's identity as a writer. One's physical home is, as William James explains, an essential part of the self: "Its scenes are part of our life; its aspects awaken the tenderest feelings of affection; and we do not easily forgive the stranger who, in visiting it, finds fault with its arrangements or treats it with contempt" (1:280). Maggie Verver's clothes, Henry James's Lamb House: "All these different things are the objects of instinctive preferences coupled with the most important practical interests of life" (1:280).[14] Lamb House fulfills the requirements that Ruskin sets out for domestic dwellings. For Ruskin, houses should have "such differences as might suit and express each man's character and occupation, and partly his history" (8:229). Ruskin suggests that, in order for houses to fully accomplish their historical purpose, "it would be well that blank stones should be left in places, to be inscribed with a summary of his [the inhabitant's] life and of its experience, raising thus the habitation to a kind of monument" (8:229). In "Winchelsea, Rye, and 'Denis Duval,' " James, who writes his own monuments (albeit Ozymandian ones), reads Lamb House's visual appearance as a summary of the writer's history:

Even now you may see things as you stand on the edge of the cliff: best of all on the open, sunny terrace of a dear little old garden—a garden brown-walled, red-walled, rose-covered on its other sides, divided by the width of a quiet street of grass-grown cobbles from the house of its master, and possessed of a little old glass-fronted, panelled pavilion which I hold to be the special spot in the world where Thackeray might most fitly have figured out his story. There is not much room in the pavilion, but there is room for the hard-pressed table and the tilted chair—there is room for a novelist and his friends. The panels have a queer paint and a venerable slant; the small chimney-place is at your back; the south window is perfect, the privacy bright and open. (172)

Like the best American scenes, Rye supplies both a view from an elevation and a bower: the city's hilltop heights provide a prospect, while the garden offers a sheltered retreat. James perceives the scene of writing as the Arcadia for which he and Cole scanned the American landscape—a middle ground between wilderness and city, nature and civilization. He insists upon the garden room's privacy: separated from the town ("brown-walled, red-walled, rose-covered") and even detached from its house by a (quiet) street's width. Yet, hidden within this hidden place is the pavilion, which has room for an intimate group, the community of writers and readers: "the novelist and his friends." This is a spot where the soul can select its own society. Its "bright and open" privacy is displayed materially in the glass and oak walls and the tilted chair of friendship next to the hard-pressed table of the writer.[15]

The walls that surround the Lamb House garden also stand in marked contrast to the open formlessness of the American landscape.[16] By enclosing a space, they give it form and thus identity. The American construction that replaces James's Ashburton Street home in *The American Scene* is one of an indistinguishable mass of buildings that erase the past, ignore the individual, and flatten the landscape. In contrast, the enclosures of Rye provide a penetrable depth by creating an inside. As in James's successful Hudson River landscapes, deep pictorial space allows for the accumulation of history. At Lamb House, time shows its marks—the "queer paint" and "venerable slant"—and, in doing so, helps foster the quirks and peculiarities that constitute identity. The particular bent of this architecture, with its slanted panels and tilted chair, is congenial to James's inclination. Looking at Lamb House, James can study the history of his self.

> How can I tell you what old—what young—visions of visions and memories of images come back to me under the influence of this quaint receptacle, into which, by kind permission, I occasionally peep, and still more under the charm of the air and the view that, as I just said, you may enjoy, close at hand, from the small terrace? How can I tell why I always keep remembering and losing there the particular passages of some far-away foolish fiction, absorbed in extreme youth, which haunt me, yet escape me, like the echo of an old premonition? I seem to myself to have lain on the grass somewhere, as a boy, poring over an English novel of the period, presumably quite bad—for they were pretty bad then too—and losing myself in the idea of just such another scene as this. But even could I rediscover the novel I wouldn't go back to it. It couldn't have been so good as this; for this—all concrete and doomed and minimised as it is—is the real thing. (172)

With this temporally and spatially complex perceptual picture, James explores the relationships between past, present, and future and between reader, text, and writer. The Lamb House garden that James sees sometimes from the outside and sometimes from within is, like Maggie's storeroom, an image for the "quaint receptacle" of his own mind. The writer's perception of this physical garden triggers a mental image of another, a garden of the past in which the youthful James lies on the grass and reads a book. A wall of brick separates the observer from the first garden; the wall of time, from the second. However, despite their division, inside and outside, past and present, reflect one another. "Old" and "young" are syntactically equated ("what old—what young"). James in the present tries to hear "the echo of an old premonition": he strains toward the past, which strains toward the present. In case we should have any doubt that the wall that separates the garden from the world and the past from the present is a mirror,[17] James tells us that what the boy reads on the page evokes a mental image of the Lamb House garden.

What this garden cluster of images illustrates is that Jamesian time follows a serpentine path. James's external and internal pictures of the gardens at Lamb House display our ability to loop back in time, to remember selectively, to choose our associations. While the past may predict the present (Lamb House's identity as the habitation of, and image for, the adult novelist originates in the boy reader of novels), the mature James's power to *re*create his youth means that neither the present Lamb House nor its Master is limited to the past: "It couldn't have been so good as this." As in the short story that bears its name, the Jamesian "real thing" is a text.[18] For James in 1901, the "real" past is not his youth, but his present pictorial reconstruction of that youth. In choosing the "concrete and doomed and minimised" garden of the present, James echoes his *American Scene* decision to move beyond the Edenic realm of "the American classic temple . . . the cult of the Indian canoe, of Fenimore Cooper, of W. C. Bryant, of the immortal water-fowl" to a postlapsarian sight, to a recognition of death's place in Arcadia. In his visual construction of the place that is his self, James acknowledges historicity, and with it, mortality.

The "passages" at the center of this garden design mark it as literary as well as temporal. James's rhetoric—the questions, qualifications ("remembering and losing"; "haunt me, yet escape me"), and tentativeness ("seem to myself"; "presumably quite bad")—insists on the limits of his knowledge. Just as the past endures into the present only as fragments that we select and reconstruct, the author survives only in the texture of his texts. One of the histories that haunts the landscapes of Winchelsea and Rye and the pages of *Denis Duval* is Thackeray's own: "What *could* he—yes—have been thinking of? . . . Thackeray carried the mystery to his grave" (168–69). James cannot extract the figure from the carpet. The written page bars direct access to the writer. Like the Jamesian walls that simultaneously separate and structure the relations between private and public, past and present, the texts of *Denis Duval* and "Winchelsea, Rye, and 'Denis Duval' " are not permeable, but readable.

We cannot extract Henry James from his essay, but we can trace in its final pages his homely visual construction of a self. Admitting that the Rye landscape appears "dreary" in comparison to Winchelsea's "classic, academic note, the note of Turner and Claude" (176), James wishes that Rye were a few feet higher, then corrects himself: "But that way depression lies, and the humiliation of those moments at which the brooding spectator says to himself that both tower and hill *would* have been higher if the place had only been French or Italian. Its whole pleasant little pathos, in point of fact, is just that it is homely English" (177). Punningly identifying himself with the lowly landscape ("that way depression lies"), James locates his home.[19] The Rye that one can offer "to show" the visitor from the theatrical heights of Ellen Terry's Winchelsea house may appear lowly: "From the garden of the distinguished cottage, at any rate, it is a large, melancholy view" (176); but this distanced perception represents the tourist's quick consumption of a picturesque "show." Sharing no history with the scene, such a perceiver resembles William James's visiting stranger who treats our home with contempt or the speeding railroad traveler of *The American Scene*. Living at Rye over time, one perceives differently. As William James explains, "Our own things are *fuller* for us than those of others because of the memories they awaken and the practical hopes and expectations they arouse" (1:311). "Those who love it," who share a history with Rye, have waited to see the landscape at its "best hour," in the right "conditions of atmosphere," and do so from "a friendly eminence that stands nearer" (176–77). The passage of time makes the landscape regal: "covered by the westering sun, [it] gives out the full measure of its old browns that turn to red and its old reds that turn to purple" (177). Penetrating into this softly colored eastern landscape, the loving perceiver will see Romney Marsh "mellowed to mere russet at the far end, and other obscure charms, revealed best to the slow cyclist, scattered over its breast: little old 'bits' that are not to be described, yet are known, with a small thrill, when seen; little lonely farms, red and gray, little mouse-coloured churches; little villages that seem made only for long shadows and summer afternoons. Brookland, Old Romney, Ivychurch, Dymchurch, Lydd—they have positively the prettiest names" (177). James takes a slow, circling, visual excursion into and about the landscape that resembles his stroll into the Saco Valley in *The American Scene*. He is figured in the landscape, not only as "the slow cyclist," but also in the details of its pattern. James's history as resident is traceable in this intimate view: his trained "painter's eye" identifies " 'bits' "; he recognizes the towns (William James's "labels") and, as a writer, collects their names.[20] If "Winchelsea, Rye, and 'Denis Duval' " begins as James's visual attempt to identify his historical relation to Thackeray, it ends with his perceptual construction of a literary habitat.

"Within the Rim"

James's pictures of England in the 1914 essay "Within the Rim" are less comforting.[21] Confronted with the First World War, James needs to insist on the connections between past and present in order to reassure himself that there will be a future, that England will remain England, and that he will remain Henry James. James's position throughout "Within the Rim" is the mirror image of Maggie's in *The Golden Bowl*. Despite Maggie's attempts to preserve the recognizable identities of her father, friend, husband, and self, *The Golden Bowl*'s emphasis is on her effort to gain freedom by shattering the logic of consistency between past and present, present and future. In "Within the Rim" the emphasis is reversed. For James in 1914 the loss of the past, and with it the loss of identity, is a more immanent threat than the prison of a fixed self.

No longer strolling easily into the landscape, James takes up Maggie's anxious pace, stalking along England's rim, the ramparts of Rye. His channel perceptions of the English landscape are informed by views of France and Belgium, which he attempts simultaneously to see and to avoid. In 1914, James's eye is more interested than ever as he scrutinizes the landscape, focusing on idiosyncratically English details, attempting to compose familiar scenes. He searches visually for structures that will order an experiential world that threatens to disintegrate into chaos, dissolving with it the self formed by experience.

As William James explains, forms and genres order our experience, structures inform our perceptions—"If we read 'no more' we expect presently to come upon a 'than' " (1:245); we are aware of "that shadowy scheme of the 'form' of an opera, play, or book, which remains in our mind and on which we pass judgment when the actual thing is done" (1:246–47); "our notion of a scientific or philosophical system" organizes the information we receive from our environment (1:247). In "Winchelsea, Rye, and 'Denis Duval,' " James orders his perceptions of the two towns by focusing on walled enclosures. Strether composes his first sight of Marie de Vionnet by resorting to the category of "lady." The Hudson River paintings of James's past provide a similar structure in *The American Scene*.

These are narrative structures, as James's American landscapes make clear. Such narrativity becomes the explicit topic of visual analysis in "Within the Rim." Attempting in 1914 to see a landscape visibly continuous over time, James explores how we shape our experience into narrative. England's "land and water and sky" constitute "a wondrous story" (17); the possible erasure of such scenes is, for James, the loss of a tale:

> When once the question fairly hung there of the possibility, more showily set forth than it had up to then presumed to be, of a world without use for the tradition so embodied, an order substituting for this, by an unmannerly thrust, quite another and really, it would seem, quite a ridiculous, a crudely and clumsily improvised story, we might all have resembled together a group of children at their nurse's knee disconcerted by some tale that it isn't their habit to hear. We loved the old tale, or at least I did, exactly because I knew it. (31)

The "tradition" that is "embodied" by James's perceptual picture is an integrity of identity. "England" has been a known narrative, a familiar story. James's cozy figure illustrates how his readable landscape, by telling the same story over time, connects his youth with his age. Despite the comforting nature of this description, James's longing for the England that he knows is not the desire to escape history, but an attempt to encounter it. An identity that is narrative can incorporate consistency *and* change. William James explains that, in the face of ever-changing appearances, we identify phenomena by recognizing "resemblance" and "continuity." These are precisely the same grounds whereby the "I" identifies a "me": "*The sense of our own personal identity, then, is exactly like any one of our other perceptions of sameness among phenomena. It is a conclusion grounded either on the resemblance in a fundamental respect, or on the continuity before the mind, of the phenomena compared*" (1:318). It is also, as "Winchelsea, Rye, and 'Denis Duval' " illustrates, a conclusion that rests on the ability to remember. Such a definition of identity allows for, indeed embraces, variation over time: "It must not be . . . treated as a sort of metaphysical or absolute Unity in which all differences are overwhelmed" (1:318). William James acknowledges freely that an identity of this sort is "relative" (1:352); what he is describing is *the experience of identity*. Historical, contingent, and personal, both "Henry James" and Henry James's "England" are just such experienced identities.

This Jamesian visual "tale" of England is an unbroken narrative. In contrast, the "crudely and clumsily improvised story" that threatens to replace it is badly formed and without precedent. Rather than a new twist in the continuing narrative that James knows as England, World War I seems a historical break. The war disturbs James's relations with language. He complains that he cannot bring himself to write fiction.[22] Attempting to describe the American Volunteer Motor Ambulance Corps's task in an interview, he laments, "The war has used up words; they have weakened, they have deteriorated like motor car tires; they have, like millions of other things, been more overstrained and knocked about and voided of the happy semblance during the last six months than in all the long ages before."[23] The war has emptied words of their representational power ("voided of the happy semblance"). Referring only to itself, language becomes nonfunctional, the tires go flat. Michael Fried and Walter Benn Michaels have argued that "a thematics of 'the *materiality* of writing,' is . . . one of the most urgent concerns of artistic representation in the half-century between the end of the Civil War and the beginning of World War I."[24] As Fried points out, "Were that materiality allowed to come unimpededly to the surface, not only would the very possibility of narrative continuity be lost, the writing in question would cease to *be* writing and would become mere mark."[25] This is precisely the situation James faces in the early days of the Great War: words have deteriorated into marks.

The fullness of language that James seeks to recover is not some timeless, unchanging identity between words and world; indeed, it is precisely the historicity of language that is under investigation. For flatness not only figures the failure of signification and, with it, the impossibility of narrative continuity; it also, as in *The American Scene*, signals the loss of the past. The rapid changes and erasures in the American landscape repeatedly thwarted James's attempts to retain his American self; the discontinuity in England's identity threatens him with an aphasia both verbal and visual. In the *Principles*, William James recounts an aphasiac's description of his condition which renders with uncanny clarity Henry's dilemma:

> "I was suddenly seized with a visual trouble infinitely more pronounced. Objects grew small and receded to infinite distances—men and things together. . . . *The world was escaping from me.* . . . I remarked at the same time that my voice was extremely far away from me, that it sounded no longer as if mine. . . . In addition to being so distant, objects appeared to me *flat.* . . . There was inside of me a new being, and another part of myself, the old being, which took no interest in the new-comer. . . . I had an ardent desire to see my old world again, to get back to my old self." (1:357)[26]

"Within the Rim" begins with James's attempt to see his old world again, to get back his old self. He seeks to make sense of his reaction to World War I by recalling his experience of the American Civil War. James's "recognition" of this resemblance implies a contiguity between the past and the present, between the world in which the Civil War took place and the one in which the Great War has begun, between the young and the old James (13). However, James finds that "the rich analogy, the fine and sharp identity between the faded and the vivid case broke down . . . experience felt the ground give way and that one swung off into space, into history, into darkness, with every lamp extinguished and every abyss gaping" (13–14). The facts that face James in 1914 are so alien that they threaten to demolish the structures of the past, to begin history anew. The result would be an unbridgeable gap between past and present that would leave James in what his brother calls "one great blooming, buzzing confusion"—the bewildering environment of the newborn child who is without a stock of experiential categories (1:462). Henry James's own vivid description of his plight recalls Cole's *Expulsion from the Garden of Eden*. But, unlike Adam, James may not even be able to find his footing in the fallen world of history and narrative. Without a precedent on which to stand, James may plunge further, swinging into a dark, formless abyss where neither the self nor its environment retains the consistent structures that make for identity.

At Rye, even the most familiar aspects of his world threaten to escape James: "Round about him stretched the scene of his fondest frequentation as time had determined the habit; but it was as if every reason and every sentiment conducing to the connection had, under the shock of events, entered into solution with every other, so that the only thinkable approach to rest, that is to the recovery of an inward order, would be in restoring them each, or to as many as would serve the purpose, some individual dignity and some form" (17–18). This is one of James's regular walks, but he can no longer see the landscape "as time had determined the habit." The perceptual practices that, in the past, made the scene into an assumed backdrop have been broken by the "shock of events." James's picture of Rye, once "taken for granted," is now "exposed to some fresh and strange and strong determinant": the hidden scene across the channel (18).[27] Such a break in England's Jamesian story constitutes a breakdown in the "inward order," the pattern of associations that identifies James himself. His associations become jumbled together, disordering the picture. Instead of taking his usual visual shortcut, he must deliberately trace the path of his associations.

If, as William James argues, *"habit diminishes the conscious attention with which our acts are performed"* (1:119), the disruption of habit forces us into self-consciousness. Like Maggie, when threatened, James seeks to preserve the forms of the past by seeing self-consciously. However, James's perceptual pictures also resemble Maggie's in that the added factor of self-aware-ness *changes* his relationship to the past. He must rearrange, must begin a "reparatory, re-identifying process" (18). "In face of what during those horrible days seemed exactly over the way the old inviolate England, as to whom the fact that she *was* inviolate, in every valid sense of the term, had become, with long acquaintance, so common and dull, suddenly shone in a light never caught before and which was for the next weeks, all the magnificence of August and September, to re-duce a thousand things to a sort of merciless distinctness" (21). If James's historical and geographic positions make him vul-nerable to verbal and visual aphasia, it is nonetheless precisely his location in time and space that directs his renewed attention to the landscape. Standing on England's vulnerable rim, aware of both England's historical inviolacy and the recent violation of other countries' coastlines, he becomes visually aware of the physical facts that underlie what had become an unex-amined verbal cliché: the "insularity" of "old inviolate England." "'Insularity!'—one had spent no small part of one's past time in mocking or in otherwise fingering the sense out of that word; yet here it was in the air wherever one looked and as stuffed with meaning as if nothing had ever worn away from it" (23). Worn away like a childhood toy (or a flat tire), "insularity" has become flattened into a mere mark. Yet the word acquires a renewed fullness of meaning when James literally sees that an insular landscape is an island: "Just the fixed *look* of England under the August sky. . . . That appearance was of the exempt state, the record of long safe centuries, in its happiest form" (24).[28]

James's visual recognition of England's insularity might seem to imply that he is asserting an Emersonian identity of signifier, signified, and referent: words are the signs of natural facts which are the symbols of spiritual facts. Jamesian words are, however, like Jamesian perceptions, and like "James" himself, provisional and historical: "What the term [*insularity*] essentially signified was in the oddest way a question at once enormous and irrelevant; what it might *show* as signifying, what it was in the circumstances actively and most probably going to, seemed rather the true consideration, indicated with all the weight of the evidence scattered about" (24). Rather than natural verbal and perceptual signs for the essential England, both the word insular and the island's visual appearance exist for James "in the circumstances"—in a particular environment, at a specific moment. "Insularity" has, in the past, meant "provincial," but in 1914 James realizes that, like the wall that separates Lamb House from the world, England's enclosing coastline fosters the growth of individual traits. Reading the visual record of England's insularity, James sees that her island identity lies in local detail: "She was pouring forth this identity, as atmosphere and aspect and picture" (25). James attempts throughout *The American Scene* to employ the Hudson River painters' combination of local detail with classical forms as a means of perceptually controlling America's rapid change, its flattening of the time-marked and the individual into an ahistorical, indistinguishable mass. In "Winchelsea, Rye, and 'Denis Duval,'" the walled Lamb House garden appears as a place for the growth of the personal and the particular. In 1914, James focuses on the way England's island boundaries have, like those of Darwin's Galapagos, created "felt idiosyncrasies" (25). "The particulars of one's affection, the more detailed the better—the blades of grass, the outlines of leaves, the drift of clouds, the streaks of mortar between old bricks, not to speak of the call of child-voices muffled in the comforting air, became, as I have noted, with a hundred other like touches, casually felt, extraordinary admonitions and symbols, close links of a tangible chain" (31). James's affection for, and attention to, these details allows him to weave them together in a "tangible chain" that is both the patterned landscape and the associations that order it.[29] Acutely aware of the island border on which he stands, James focuses on edges and outlines. As always, he searches actively for visible signs of human history: here, the traces of past workers written in mortar, thinned by time. The future, embodied in the children, he cannot see. Looking into and about the landscape, James understands what the war threatens: the details that give the landscape its identity as well as the self that, in perceiving, composes that identity, England and James.

Insularity makes for identity, not only in promoting individuality, but also by marking difference. As William James explains, we define our selves by drawing a line: "One great splitting of the whole universe into two halves is made by each of us," the division into " '*me*' and '*not-me*.' . . . The neighbor's me falls together with all the rest of things in one foreign mass, against which his own *me* stands out in startling relief" (1:278).[30] In isolating the island of the self, we resemble Henry James's narrative artist: "Really, universally, relations stop nowhere, and the exquisite problem of the artist is eternally but to draw, by a geometry of his own, the circle within which they shall happily *appear* to do so" (*AN*, 5). An identity that lies in difference is dependent; the " '*me*' " is defined by the " '*not-me.*' " In "Within the Rim," England's boundaries stand out visibly against "the immediate presence, as it were, of France and Belgium," countries whose borders have proved permeable (15). "Insularity" deconstructs. England appears to James as her "old inviolate" self precisely because the island is threatened with violation. "Wouldn't it be the thing supremely in character that England should look most complacently herself, irradiating all her reasons for it, at the very crisis of the question of the true toughness, in other words the further duration, of her identity?" (24–25).

In focusing on England's insular details and the rim that marks the island's boundaries, James attempts visually to hold off the penetration that leads to dissolution. But the strategy works for only two more years. For the dying Henry James, the boundaries of the self dissolve. In his final dictations he becomes what he has read, writing himself as Napoleon. It is as though William James's famous example of the continuity of the stream of thought—"When Peter and Paul wake up in the same bed, and recognize that they have been asleep, each one of them mentally reaches back and makes connection with but *one* of the two streams of thought which were broken by the sleeping hours" (1:232)—goes awry. Only by awakening as another self, a royal "we," can Henry James return words to their fullness: "Wondrous enough certainly to have a finger in such a concert and to feel ourselves touch the large old phrase into the right amplitude. It had shrunken."[31]

However, in 1914 James is still able to perceive a place in the English landscape for his Anglo-American identity:

> Technical alien as he was, the privilege of the great partaking, of shared instincts and ideals, of a communion of

> race and tongue, temper and tradition, put on before all
> the blest appearances a splendour to which I hoped that
> so long as I might yet live my eyes would never grow
> dim. And the great intensity, the melting together of the
> spiritual sources so loosed in a really intoxicating draught,
> was when I shifted my watch from near east to far west
> and caught the enemy. (34–35)

The "blest appearances" of James's Rye view make him aware
of what he shares with the English. Standing within that landscape, James turns west to face a puzzling mental image of the
land where he is still citizen. The threat to England that Ger-
many's invasion of Belgium poses so affects James that he sees
America invaded by the German army. Being an American
citizen makes James a "technical alien," yet, at the same time,
the past that America shares with England ("shared instincts
and ideals," "race and tongue, temper and tradition") means
that being an American also allows James to be English, to
engage in the war, to catch the enemy. As his western picture
shows, for James, the two countries are united.

Like Maggie's mental images, Jamess, is predictive. His visual assertion of dual citizenship here helps to explain why, less
than six months later, he declares himself a British subject. In
"Within the Rim," James acknowledges lightly that he is a
"technical alien." Yet, in a half-year's time, what these words
"*show* as signifying" is that in order to travel to Lamb House
from London he must register with the authorities. The historical circumstances of the war force James to be solely American, rather than American and British.[32] After his years in
England, such a label makes James alien to himself. By becoming a British subject, he is, as he explains to his nephew
Harry, "making my civil status merely agree not only with
my moral, but with my material as well, in every kind of
way. . . . I have spent here all the best years of my life—they
practically have *been* my life."[33] The "material" facts of James's

English residence—the experiential history that he shares with his environment—have worked to create an "absolute need and passion."[34] In and through his pictures of the English landscape James has identified himself—as adult, as writer, as member of a literary community, formed over time, and as a writer and reader of visible history. England is the body of his past.

Notes

1. Stephen Bann, "The Sense of the Past: Image, Text, and Object in the Formation of Historical Consciousness in Nineteenth-Century Britain," in *The New Historicism*, ed. H. Aram Veeser (New York: Routledge, 1989), 104.

2. Later in his discussion of Winchelsea, James notes with relief that the church is "mercifully exempt as yet from restoration" (171). In *The Seven Lamps of Architecture*, Ruskin defines *restoration* as "the most total destruction which a building can suffer" (8:242). This abhorrence of restoration stemmed partly from the awful results of many nineteenth-century restoration projects. Ancient buildings were "purified" and "corrected" by architects whose knowledge of earlier styles and techniques was sketchy and distorted.

3. For the relationship between ruins and literary fragments, see Thomas McFarland, *Romanticism and the Forms of Ruin: Wordsworth, Coleridge, and Modalities of Fragmentation* (Princeton: Princeton University Press, 1981). Balachandra Rajan, *The Form of the Unfinished: English Poetics from Spenser to Pound* (Princeton: Princeton University Press, 1985), 4–5, argues that an unfinished fragment cannot be equated with a ruin because the former was never a finished whole. However, James's professional tendency to rewrite as he reads leads him to regard fragments as potentially completable works. On James's literary interest in gaps and indeterminacies, see Paul B. Armstrong, *The Challenge of Bewilderment: Understanding and Representation in James, Conrad, and Ford* (Ithaca: Cornell University Press, 1987), 17–19.

4. For a history of this interpretation and its variations, see Laurence Goldstein, *Ruins and Empire: The Evolution of a Theme in Augustan and Romantic Literature* (Pittsburgh: University of Pittsburgh Press, 1977). For other discussions of ruins in James, see John Carlos Rowe's analysis of "Travelling Companions," in *The Theoretical Dimensions*

of Henry James (Madison: University of Wisconsin Press, 1984), 199–201, and Elissa Greenwald, "The Ruins of Empire: Reading the Monuments in Hawthorne and James," *CEA Critic* 46 (Spring–Summer 1984): 48–59.

5. In the Preface to *The American*, James describes his early anxiety about serial publication, citing the "sad warning" of *Denis Duval*, Mrs. Gaskell's *Wives and Daughters*, and Robert Louis Stevenson's *The Weir of Hermiston*, novels left unfinished because of the deaths of their respective authors (*AC*, 271).

6. Letter to Edmund Gosse, 25 August 1915 (4:776).

7. On the possibility that consciousness survives death, see Henry James, "Is There a Life After Death?" *Harper's Bazar* 44 (January, February 1910): 26, 128–29.

8. James's uneasiness about his survival is hinted at in "Winchelsea, Rye, and 'Denis Duval'" when he mentions that he has given Thackeray's book its "final reading" (163) and when he refers in passing to Longfellow's "fine verses on the death of the Duke of Wellington" (165). The reference is to the 1852 "The Warden of the Cinque Ports," whose last stanza reads:

> Meanwhile, without, the surly cannon waited,
> The sun rose bright o'erhead;
> Nothing in Nature's aspect intimated
> That a great man was dead.

9. See "The Novels of George Eliot": "In every novel the work is divided between the writer and the reader; but the writer makes the reader very much as he makes his characters" (*HJLC* 2:922).

10. James's insistence here on loyalty is echoed in his other late writings on authors whom he has read for a lifetime. In the reviews of his youth, James is most critical of those writers whose influence over him is greatest. However, in the retrospectives and commemorations of his maturity, he finds that any weaknesses in these writers' works is outweighed by his affection for the writers themselves. See, for example, his remarks on George Eliot in *The Middle Years*, collected in *Henry James: Autobiography*, ed. Frederick W. Dupee (1956; reprint, Princeton: Princeton University Press, 1983), 573–74, and his comments on Zola in his 1903 essay "Emile Zola" (*AC*, 425–59).

11. See *The Biographical Edition of W. M. Thackeray's Complete Works*, ed. Mrs. Anne Thackeray Ritchie (New York and London:

Harper and Brothers, 1899). Ritchie records that her father even sketched one of the "ancient gateways" (xxv).

12. James's picture hints that the scene's visual attractions may have been perceived only once eyes had been trained by impressionist painting to see points of light and to delight in ordinary outdoor holiday making. For James's mixed feelings on impressionism, see Chapter 3.

13. This French ability to cook up an arrangement will be noted again in *The Ambassadors*, where Strether finds that in the garden of the Tuileries "the air had a taste as of something mixed with art, something that presented nature as a white-capped master-chef" (21:79). Strether goes on to engage in his own visual artistry: "The palace was gone, Strether remembered the palace; and when he gazed into the irremediable void of its site the historic sense in him might have been freely at play—the play under which in Paris indeed it so often winces like a touched nerve. He filled out spaces with dim symbols of scenes; he caught the gleam of white statues at the base of which, with his letters out, he could tilt back a straw-bottomed chair" (21:79-80).

14. In a 9 August 1899 letter, Henry James uses William's own argument to demonstrate to his skeptical older brother the absolute necessity of purchasing Lamb House. He declares that, after two years' residence, the house has come to feel like his " 'last long home' " and notes: "The extraordinary congruity of the little place with all my needs, conveniences, tastes, limitations (and even extensions), with every sort of security, salubrity and economy—and a congruity not general and approximate, but stretching into every detail and ramification" (4:114).

15. In his correspondence, James also describes Lamb House as a middle ground, emphasizing its quiet privacy, while stressing its easy accessibility to London. See also Richard Gill, *Happy Rural Seat: The English Country House and the Literary Imagination* (New Haven: Yale University Press, 1972), 92–93, for the argument that James's "quiet houses" allow for "withdrawal," not escapism.

16. See James's relief in *The American Scene* at the way the wall surrounding the Harvard Yard orders the ordinarily amorphous American landscape (62). John Carlos Rowe, *Henry Adams and Henry James: The Emergence of a Modern Consciousness* (Ithaca: Cornell University Press, 1976), notes "the connection between the enclosure of the Harvard Yard and the aesthetic process" (159). James's first pub-

lished travel essay on England, "A European Summer. I. Chester," *The Nation*, 4 July 1872, 7–9, later published as "Chester" in *English Hours*, is virtually a paean to the English wall.

17. For a more extended analysis of another Jamesian use of this image, see my "Seeing Doubles: Reflections of the Self in James's *Sense of the Past*," *Modern Language Quarterly* 45 (March 1984): 48–60. Ellen Eve Frank interprets a scene similar to the Lamb House one quite differently in *Literary Architecture: Essays Toward a Tradition* (Berkeley: University of California Press, 1979), 190–93. She does not identify the cliffside cottage at the center of this scene (in the Preface to *The Spoils of Poynton*), but it is another Sussex landscape: "Point Hill" in Playden (see Leon Edel, *Henry James: The Treacherous Years*, 1895–1901 [Philadelphia: J. B. Lippincott, 1969], 157).

18. James's 1893 story raises the possibility that the representational is the "real."

19. See also the essay's closing lines: "But the point to be made is that, comparing small things with great—which may always be done when small things are amiable—if Rye and its rock and its church are a miniature Mont-Saint-Michel, so, when the summer deepens, the shadows fall, and the mounted shepherds and their dogs pass before you in the grassy desert, you find in the mild English 'marsh' a recall of the Roman Campagna" (177–78). What is striking in the above passage is not the similarity between England and Italy but the attributes that belong to the English landscape alone: "small"; "small"; "amiable"; "miniature"; "mild." The allusions to Mont-Saint-Michel and the Roman Campagna point the reader not to the Continent but to the writer and perceiver who "recall(s)," who carries his visual memories of those scenes back home to England.

20. James's *Notebooks* are filled with lists of likely names, many of which he went on to use in his fiction. The identification of James as the "slow cyclist" above accords with the fact that he was an avid bicyclist in the nineties.

21. By 1911 the aging James had found Rye winters too lonely. In a 27 October 1911 letter to Theodora Bosanquet, he described "bolting—in horror and loathing . . . from Rye for the winter" (4:589).

22. See, for example, his letter to Rhoda Broughton, 10 August 1914 (4:713–14).

23. Preston Lockwood, "Henry James's First Interview," *New York Times Magazine*, 21 March 1915, 4.

24. Walter Benn Michaels, *The Gold Standard and the Logic of Naturalism: American Literature at the Turn of the Century* (Berkeley: University of California Press, 1987), 21. Michaels is quoting Michael Fried, *Realism, Writing, Disfiguration: On Thomas Eakins and Stephen Crane* (Chicago: University of Chicago Press, 1987), xiii.

25. Fried, *Realism, Writing, Disfiguration*, xiv.

26. The case is taken from an account in Hippolyte Taine's *On Intelligence*. Henry James was quite familiar with much of Taine's writing and reviewed a number of his works, not including, however, *On Intelligence*.

27. This same insistent coupling of the two channel landscapes recurs in James's correspondence. See James's remarkably similar descriptions of what he sees from his position "within the rim" in letters to Rhoda Broughton, 10 August 1914 (4:713–14); Edith Wharton, 19 August 1914 (4:715–16); Brander Matthews, 22 August 1914 (4:716–18); and Mrs. Thomas Sergeant Perry, 22 September 1914 (4:718–19).

28. As Ruth Bernard Yeazell astutely points out, "A fascination with concealed meanings lurking in well-worn phrases, with dramatic plots which suddenly emerge from cliché metaphors, runs in fact through all late Jamesian prose—nonfiction as well as fiction" (*Language and Knowledge in the Late Novels of Henry James* [Chicago: University of Chicago Press, 1976], 31).

29. Despite their consistent uses of the model of the stream, both Henry and William James occasionally refer to the "chain" of association. As this case illustrates, the use of the term does not indicate a reversion to the older, passive model for the mind, with its "units" of thought.

30. George Eliot describes the necessity of this split in *Middlemarch*, Cabinet Edition, 3 vols. (Edinburgh and London: William Blackwood, 1878–80): "If we had a keen vision and feeling of all ordinary human life, it would be like hearing the grass grow and the squirrel's heart beat, and we should die of that roar which lies on the other side of silence" (1: 297–98).

31. *Notebooks of Henry James*, ed. Leon Edel and Lyall Powers (New York: Oxford University Press, 1987), 582.

32. The United States' resistance to entering the conflict that had already engaged England so deeply made it all the clearer to James that the two countries were not one.

33. Letter to Henry James III, 24 June 1915 (4:760).

34. Ibid., 761.

Index

Page numbers in italics indicate illustrations.

History: American landscape as site of, 22, 92–94, 101–39, 144n38; in Claude Lorrain's landscapes, 107, 110, 120; discontinuity in 18–19, 23–24, 88n21, 92, 94–95, 104–5, 110, 128, 149, 151, 165–75; English landscape as site of, 23, 92, 149–64; the fall into, 128, 130–32, 144n39, 149, 162, 169; in Hudson River paintings, 92–93, 104–10, 118–19, 171–72; in Cole's work, 94, 121–30, 132, 154, 169. *See also* Depth; Language; Narrative

Hocks, Richard A., 7, 25n14, 26n21, 28n37, 44, 53, 55n7, 55n12, 56n21, 85n1, 140n8

Holland, J. Gill, 54n3

Holland, Laurence, 84, 145n48

Holly, Carol, 21

Hudson River school: atmosphere in, 22, 107, 115, 118–19; as "childish," 105–6; Claude Lorrain's influence on, 107, 110, 118; depth in, 22, 93, 99, 106–10, 118–19; and Henry James's childhood, 21, 93, 95–96, 104–6, 166; Henry James's use of, 21–22, 93–96, 99, 104–7, 110–12, 117–19, 143–44n36, 159–61, 171–72; as historical, 92–93, 104–10, 118–19, 171–72; light in, 105, 107, 117–19; local detail in, 99, 110, 117–19, 141n20, 171–72; Ruskin's influence on, 21, 99. *See also* Durand, Asher; Iridescence

Hudson, William, P., 27n27

Hume, David, 10, 15, 37

Husserl, Edmund, 5

Impressionism: in Henry James's landscapes, 112–15, 142n31; literary, 31n53, 61, 142–43nn31,32; in painting, 112–13, 142n30, 177n12. *See also* Postimpressionism

Inattention, 49, 56n16, 66–67, 88n18, 115–17. *See also* Attention

Inconsistency, as freedom in *The Golden Bowl,* 70–71, 88n21, 165. *See also* Discontinuity; Fragments

Inness, George: *The Lackawanna Valley,* 142n27

Iridescence, 22, 101–2, 111–12, 142n29. *See also* Atmosphere; Depth; Light

Irving, Washington, 110, 120–21.

Irving, Washington, Works: "The Legend of Sleepy Hollow," 111, 139; "Rip Van Winkle," 95–97, 139

Iser, Wolfgang, 145n48

James, Henry: as aesthete, 3, 14, 29–30n47; American citizenship, 139, 174–75; childhood and Hudson River school, 21, 93, 95–96, 104–6, 166; personal relations with William James, 6–7; and his reading of William James's work, 6–8, 26n20

James, Henry, Works: *The Ambassadors,* 19–20, 29n41, 33–54, 57–62, 64, 84–85, 89n27, 93, 112, 154–55, 166, 177n13; *The American Scene,* 21–23, 91–139, 149, 151, 154, 160–62, 164, 166, 171–72; "The Art of Fiction," 24n2; "The Beast in the Jungle," 76; "Emile Zola," 176n10; "A European Summer. I. Chester," 177–78n16; "The